Praise for

THE HIDDEN POWER OF THE FIVE HEARTS

Kimberly is an amazing woman. She is brilliant.
— **Drew Barrymore**

Kimberly's philosophy reveals that the mental, emotional and spiritual aspects of you, your diet and health are one.
— **Deepak Chopra**

Kimberly is a most important heart-based teacher of our time, and the wisdom and science around the heart she offers in The Hidden Power of the Five Hearts *are utterly necessary for humanity to thrive—and survive—in this modern age.*
— **Alberto Villoldo Ph.D.**, medical anthropologist and bestselling author of *Shaman, Healer, Sage* and *Grow a New Body*.

Kimberly Snyder's HeartAlign Meditation and her teachings and insights are effective and illuminating tools to help people everywhere tap into the power of their hearts and transform their lives. Her new book, The Hidden Power of the Five Hearts, *is a magnificent guide that will help you discover the purpose, clarity, greater health, unconditional love, and peace that is within us all. I urge you not just to read this book but to study and practice its wisdom.*
— **Michael Bernard Beckwith**, founder and CEO of Agape International Spiritual Center, author of *Life Visioning* and *Spiritual Liberation* and host of *Take Back Your Mind* podcast

Kimberly's teachings on heart-based living and the HeartAlign Meditation are powerful tools to help create more peace and unity, starting within each of us and spreading across families and the world. Her work is so important and needed today.
— **Dr. Shefali Tsabary**, *New York Times* bestselling author of *The Conscious Parent*

Kimberly Snyder's teachings on heart intelligence and her heart-based HeartAlign Meditation are groundbreaking tools to promote health, vitality, emotional intelligence and happiness from within. Her new book, The Hidden Power of the Five Hearts, *is an eye-opening and fascinating read on the true power of the human heart.*
— **Dan Buettner**, founder of the Blue Zones and #1 *New York Times* best-selling author of the Blue Zones book series

In The Hidden Power of the Five Hearts, *Kimberly Snyder has an alternative to thinking harder: feel harder. This new book is an exploration of the power of the heart to reduce stress and overwhelm, transmute negative energy into vibrancy, and help us live a life of purpose. The book bridges science and spirituality in a manner that is equally insightful and useful. I am honored to call her a friend and mentor.*
— **Jeff Krasno**, CEO of Commune Media

Kimberly's teachings and the HeartAlign Meditation have profoundly positively impacted my life personally, helping me tune in to a new source of power, softness, and knowing that all stems from my heart. Her teaching merges ancient spiritual wisdom with cutting-edge technology that can benefit everyone. Kimberly is a source of light in this world and her teachings a beacon of hope for the future of humanity and the planet.
— **Casey Means, M.D.**, Levels co-founder and author of the #1 *New York Times* bestseller *Good Energy*

The Hidden Power of the Five Hearts *is much more than a book to read, it's an opportunity and an invitation to embark on a fantastic journey to better understand how to think, love, live healthier, and achieve abundance in all its forms. Kimberly Snyder is a trusted voice and authentic guide who unlocks a fascinating secret to self-empowerment heart intelligence.*
— **Thomas M. Kostigen**, multiple *New York Times* best-selling author, including *Cool Food: Erasing Your Carbon Footprint One Bite at a Time* co-authored with Robert Downey, Jr.

Kimberly Snyder's work on awakening the heart is so important and timely from both a scientific and spiritual perspective. Her new book, The Hidden Power of the Five Hearts *offers highly practical and valuable ways to create growth, abundance, and true success in your life. It will have a treasured place on my bookshelf.*
— **Hitendra Wadhwa, Ph.D.**, professor at Columbia Business School, founder of the Mentora Institute, and author of *Inner Mastery, Outer Impact.*

THE HIDDEN POWER OF THE FIVE HEARTS

THE
HIDDEN
POWER OF
THE FIVE
HEARTS

Empower Your Thoughts, Balance Your Emotions,
and Unlock Vibrant Health and Abundance

KIMBERLY SNYDER

HAY HOUSE LLC
Carlsbad, California • New York City
London • Sydney • New Delhi

Published in the United States by: Hay House LLC: www.hayhouse.com® • *Published in Australia by:* Hay House Australia Publishing Pty Ltd: www .hayhouse.com.au • *Published in the United Kingdom by:* Hay House UK Ltd: www.hayhouse.co.uk • *Published in India by:* Hay House Publishers (India) Pvt Ltd: www.hayhouse.co.in

Project editor: Melody Guy
Cover design: Kathleen Lynch
Interior design: Karim J. Garcia
Interior photos/illustrations: HeartMath Institute

Cataloging-in-Publication Data
is on file at the Library of Congress

Hardcover ISBN: 978-1-4019-7726-9
E-book ISBN: 978-1-4019-7727-6
Audiobook ISBN: 978-1-4019-7728-3

10 9 8 7 6 5 4 3 2 1
1st edition, September 2024

Printed in the United States of America

This product uses responsibly sourced papers and/or recycled materials. For more information, see www.hayhouse.com.

Dedicated to:
Paramahansa Yogananda
and
Swami Sri Yukteswar Giri,
with reverence,
love, and gratitude.

CONTENTS

A NOTE TO YOU

I have a secret to share with you. Your heart—your beautiful pumping, thumping, thinking (yes thinking), smart as a whip heart—contains within it a secret intelligence that, once accessed, has the power to literally transform every aspect of your life in a relatively short amount of time. I want to say that the transformation can happen almost overnight, but I want to choose my words carefully. And yet, I have seen some amazing things happen in the last few years (more on this later) that would blow your mind—and your heart (in a good way, of course). Bottom line: I don't make the above statement lightly. And anyone who has followed me over the years knows that I'm pretty serious about the statements that I make (and for you that are new to my work, you'll soon see I have a low tolerance for BS).

This book is about tapping into your heart's intelligence and aligning it with the intelligence in your mind. You will soon learn how to do this in surprisingly simple- and yet profoundly powerful ways. And when you do so, you can experience higher levels of success and abundance, increased physical health, unwavering confidence, deeper relationships, unconditional love, emotional resilience, and a profound sense of peace and fulfillment.

Consider this. You have multiple brains. One is in your head and another is in your heart (there's also one in your gut, which we will also discuss later on). We go to school from the time we are very young and are given a road map to accessing intelligence in our brains (learn to read, learn math, write reports), but no one ever gave us a clue about what to do with the heart! This book looks to rectify that. And I will provide guidance to you through the concept of The Five Hearts. Yes, that's right—you have multiple brains and five hearts!

Okay, let me slow down a bit. Before I go on, I want to tell you a little about me and how I got to where I am now, making bold claims about some things that seem so counterintuitive to everything we've been taught.

I grew up in an okay existence in suburban Connecticut. I was labeled as "exotic" because I'm half Filipina, which made me uncomfortable because I didn't want to stand out. The far bigger issue, though, looking back as an adult, is that I didn't have any tools to deal with my big feelings and oppressive thoughts, many of which were around doubt and not feeling good enough. I developed various identities, masks I could cling to that made me feel like I was worthy. One of the most prominent identities I held on to was being "the smart one." This led to overwhelming anxiety and perfectionism. I tried to always have perfect grades, always be number one. My sense of self was completely wrapped up in what others thought of me, and it was debilitating.

After high school, I went to college, graduated, and a few days after that graduation, I left home to work overseas and then went backpacking for about three years. I traveled all over the world—from camping across 13 countries in eastern and southern Africa, to taking trains around India, to riding horses across Mongolia.

I was trying to figure out what life was all about. I was also trying to discover a way to relieve the extreme anxiety, chronic insomnia, bloating, and restlessness I had experienced for years. I was seeking peace, but I didn't yet have a clue how to find it.

I started on a wellness path in nutrition. Over the years it's really expanded as I have seen more clearly how the different parts of us, the different energies, can work in harmony with each other. A healthy body influences a healthy mind, a healthy mind influences a healthy body, and a healthy lifestyle influences a healthy mind and a healthy spirit. Over the years I've worked as a holistic wellness coach and nutritionist, guiding my clients' diets, lifestyles, emotional well-being, and meditation practices, helping all types of people, from celebrities, movie stars, and moms and dads to young professionals, students, and retirees. It turns out we are all looking for the same thing: meaning, purpose, security, an understanding of ourselves, and a solution to all the feelings of dividedness that we carry around.

It's in this experience of separation from ourselves and from others that often prevents us from achieving our goals and dreams. I know this from my own life. My heart has been broken many times. This splitting of the heart, as everyone knows, hurts. And it hurt like hell when I went through really tough breakups (especially with the one that involved my first child, who was around 18 months old at the time) or felt betrayed by a friend. But I've been fortunate enough over the last 15+ years to have engaged in so much learning, growth, and experiences that have helped me to see the strength I have inside. It is my practice that has led me to healing and an increasingly deeper connection to who I really am.

Sometimes I used some of what this book describes without knowing it. And now that I've gained a new and far deeper understanding of the heart, and how you can use your heart to align your mind, and all of your life, I feel a burning urgency, a knowing that I just have to share that wisdom with you! Hence, this book is your guide to help you intentionally lead a life full of vitality and energy, with a clear mind, a healthy body from your skin to all the parts inside, and a spirit that connects more deeply to the world around you.

Our hearts are the very center of our being. Physically, the heart is housed around the center of our spines, halfway between our guts and our brain. And it turns out that the importance of the heart has been emphasized in spiritual traditions, ancient cultures such as the Babylonians, Greeks and Egyptians, and all major religions around the world.

The heart is also the focus of exciting scientific research around coherence, which includes the communication between the heart and the brain, pivotal for health and happiness. Coherence is a way of coordinating the electromagnetic frequencies that give life to your heart and your brain. It's about living in sync. Imagine the opposite. Say, for instance you were walking down a path and you came to a fork in a road and your left leg went left and your right leg would go right. What would happen? You'd probably split your pants or worse yet hurt yourself, but that is how our hearts and minds operate a lot of the times! Coherence is a way of bringing those two parts of you together so you can go where you want to go.

Central to this book is the big revelation: Your heart possesses an unparalleled intelligence that your mind alone could never give you access to, that can transform every aspect of your life. This is true for both your physical, tangible, beating heart, and also your spiritual heart, which is an energetic power center, a gateway to connect you to your True Self, where your humanness and Spirit merge.

When I started incorporating the power of the heart, both from the science and energetic knowledge I was discovering, everything in my life—and I do mean *everything*—went through a major upgrade. I started to have a lot more energy throughout the day, but especially at the end of the day, when I would often be spent and emotionally frazzled. I started feeling far more peaceful, even around people I used to find greatly challenging. Even my hair started to grow in thicker and healthier. Chronic pain in my hips and neck resolved. In my daily life, I still have some moments of heaviness, when I fall into old patterns, and yet overall I truly feel so much lighter and happier! The seeking out there was over, for I realized the heart is right here, right inside of each and every single one of us.

I started to bring the heart into my client work and to those around me, and I started to see massive improvements as well. I witnessed people's whole energy and lives change. And it was all happening in a nonlinear way. Meaning that, as the heart turned on a kind of intuitive and highly intelligent power inside of each person, old blocks and patterns that had been an issue for years were now being blasted through, sometimes immediately!

My team at my company, Solluna, ran a study on a heart-based practice called the HeartAlign Meditation (more on this in the following chapters) with the HeartMath Institute, an organization in California that has been studying the science of heart-brain communication and the relationship between the physical heart and the energetic or spiritual heart for over 30 years. The study results showed a 29 percent increase in coherence in just four weeks.

The heart has a way of clearing things out by providing a brand new point of view, versus the sticky and often long, roundabout way of the mind, which involves rehashing and trying to wade through the gunk.

For instance, I saw:

- People who had been struggling with weight for years simply shed off those extra pounds—with ease. This is because their hearts helped them heal the root attachment of using food to soothe big emotions.

- Chronically angry people find a way to consistent calmness.

- Overwhelmed moms find a newfound sense of centeredness and purpose.

- High-performers learn to prevent most stress entirely, versus trying to minimize its incredibly harmful effects *after* they had already gone into a stress response.

- Many people bring their creative ideas into the world in thriving, lucrative ways.

During my research, I came across a book called *The Holy Science* that had a huge impact on me. It was written by the revered monk and mystic Swami Sri Yukteswar, guru to Paramahansa Yogananda, who brought yoga to the West. While Sri Yukteswar appeared and acted sternly, it was also said that he possessed unparalleled wisdom as well as the love of a thousand mothers.

I found the section of his book where Sri Yukteswar discusses the five states of the human heart particularly captivating. He explains that we all progress through five stages of heart awakening, leading to a full realization of our true selves. Each stage brings a unique level of consciousness, shaping the reality we experience and unlocking more of our innate potential. I devoted many months to deep contemplation, immersing myself in the study of the heart and Sri Yukteswar's teachings, striving to fully understand and internalize the profound insights into the heart's mysteries.

It was during this time that I had first connected with the HeartMath Institute, starting with a podcast exchange with Deborah Rozman, PhD., the president of HeartMath. I then visited their center in Northern California and met some amazing and brilliant humans who have dedicated their lives to bringing what they call *heart intelligence* and *heart awakening* to the planet, including Executive Vice President Howard Martin, Director of Research Rollin McCraty, PhD., and the founder, Doc Childre. I was blown away by all of their work.

One evening, my husband, Jon, and I sat in a dimly lit room with Doc for hours, discussing life and practicing heart meditations together. This profound, transformative experience, difficult to express in words, opened incredible feelings in my heart. Following that night and in the subsequent days, I was inspired to incorporate the scientific insights and research from the HeartMath Institute into this book, and to conduct The HeartAlign Meditation Study together with them that I mention above. Remarkably, their findings align closely with the Five Heart stages taught by Sri Yukteswar!

That all brings us here to this moment, where we're about to embark on this voyage together. As we journey through the Five Heart stages, it will be like doing metaphorical heart surgery, helping to awaken your heart's real power so you can access more of who you really are: the True Self. You will be learning about ancient teachings and science at each stage, which together will help support you in living a more heart-centered life. You can then make major leaps in your physical, mental, emotional, and spiritual health.

Even if you're facing challenging circumstances right now, tapping into your heart's intelligence can transform your life. Unlocking your heart's power is the secret to navigating your day with less stress and will grant you the clarity to handle challenges with ease and intuition. To truly be free, you need to see things differently; otherwise, you remain trapped in the same viewpoint, allowing fear to persist and hold you back.

Your heart will show you the way.

And then you too will *experience* everything that you were ever seeking—greater health; more love, peace, abundance, and clarity; more ease and less stress; more confidence and feelings of fulfillment—was right there inside of you all along.

Chapter 1

YOUR BRILLIANT HEART

For most of my life, I've been an obsessive overthinker. I've had conversations with myself in my head, thinking, judging, and scrutinizing my life and the people around me. I constantly thought about how I appeared to others: *Do I fit in? Do I look okay? Am I smart enough? Am I saying the right things?* Instead of listening to others, I thought about what I was going to say once they took a breath and paused. I thought about mistakes I made in the past and obsessively planned the next steps so I could best control the future outcomes that I wanted.

I thought so much that I was up all hours of the night and suffered severe insomnia at times. Overthinking fueled intense anxiety, and my body held incredible tension that caused chronic constipation, bloating, and digestion issues; jaw grinding, tight shoulders, hair that wouldn't grow much; acne and other skin issues; and all kinds of aches, including chronic hip and neck pain.

All this thinking was exhausting!

Thinking is important, of course. We need to think to function in life. But if we let thinking run rampant—if our minds lead our lives—confusion, depleted energy, unhappiness, low and negative thoughts, and frustration will all run rampant too. Our unbridled minds, our unmanaged egos, which we will refer to here on in as simply our egos, are like wild horses. If not tamed, they run all over the place.

Your ego can feed you thousands upon thousands of thoughts a day, many of which are simply untrue. Thoughts such as *you aren't doing enough, you don't stack up,* and the really harsh one: *you aren't good enough.* The mind is important, but it often sees things in a linear, comparative, quantifiable, and step-by-step forward approach. It has a certain kind of fact-based intelligence, but this intelligence does have limits.

What many of us don't know is that we have another mind within us, another brain if you will. And that other brain is the heart. I know it sounds like a contradiction. If I have a heart problem, I don't see a neurologist, I see a cardiologist. The heart does the pumping; the brain does the thinking.

Yet more and more scientific studies have revealed that the heart has its own form of intelligence, one that offers a clearer picture of the world around us—and the world within us. **An intelligence so vast that it is actually brilliant—and can literally change everything in our lives if we can just learn how to harness its power. And we don't just have one heart; we have five hearts. I don't mean this physically as in how we literally have two kidneys.** But there are five realities within our hearts that once accessed and understood will radically shift your view of everything in your life.

This book is about shifting your life from the mind to the heart. This means that your heart will start to lead your life, instead of your mind. This is like your heart lassoing a rope around your wild horse mind and telling it to get in line! Your mind is still important, but it's going to align with your all-powerful heart. The "lasso" represents what heart coherence is like, which is part of the heart's brilliant intelligence. This is the syncing up of the dynamic connection between your heart, brain, and nervous system. This powerful fusion will unlock profound intelligence that will enhance every facet of your life.

In the 1990s, the HeartMath Institute researchers identified a physiological state called *heart rhythm coherence*, or *heart coherence*, which occurs when our breathing, heart rate variability (HRV), and brain rhythms as well as our hormonal responses are in sync and work harmoniously together. This state is the foundation for improved health and increased energy, minimizing stress reactions and boosting our intuitive, direct "knowingness," giving us new, creative solutions and better decision-making that we simply couldn't see from our minds alone. With heart coherence, the wild horse of our minds is harnessed into better mental functioning, including more focus, improved memory, and faster reaction times.

Learning to awaken your heart and tap into its amazing power has been measured scientifically and shown to elevate your physical health, including allowing for hormonal balance and reducing strain and physical aging on your skin, heart, and other organs.[1] It means you can experience better digestion and weight management. But there's more. Much, much more.

In this chapter, we'll explore your heart's language, what your heart's extraordinary intelligence truly means, and why you can always trust your heart.

THE POWER OF YOUR HEART

Did you know that your heart actually has its own independent nervous system[2]? The heart contains 40,000 neurons, or brain-like cells that include sensory neurites, which help in receiving and transmitting information. It turns out there is a whole heart language that helps direct your brain and the rhythms in your body, and your heart sends more messages to the brain than vice versa! Your heart also creates an electromagnetic field that is a hundred times greater than the field your brain creates. So, what does this all mean?

It means that your heart is not just a muscle pumping blood through your body or a metaphor for sentimental love. *It is a center of profound intelligence.* Your heart is also a kind of brain. It is a central access point of energy, a doorway whereby you can experience who you really are and your connection to Spirit and your higher self, however you like to conceive of it.

The science was especially interesting to me because it validated what I had been studying for years in my spiritual studies. **It confirmed that our heart—not our brain as we have been led to believe—is actually the central place of our intelligence. And not just intelligence as in "pretty smart." The heart contains an** *extraordinary* **level of intelligence that is brilliant!** It pointed to a merger between science and the energetic or spiritual parts of us, revealing that our hearts are the center of our power that can help us unlock all that we seek.

What *is* heart intelligence? It's energetic, emotional, mental, spiritual, and physical. It involves creating greater heart coherence, or heart-brain alignment, and tapping into your heart's profound wisdom and allowing it to come front and center to guide your life. Doc Childre, founder of the HeartMath Institute, says, "Picture heart intelligence as the flow of awareness, understanding and intuitive guidance we experience when the mind and emotions are brought into coherent alignment with the heart."[3]

That's exactly what you are going to learn in this book. The more you dive into the tools and practices offered to you here, the more your own heart intelligence will enable you to experience extraordinary levels of intuition, creativity and flow, emotional intelligence, greater physical health, deep connection to others, fulfilling relationships, confidence within yourself, and deep levels of peace and love.

It's very practical! For instance, I can say that applying the power of The Five Hearts to my life resulted in about a 90 percent reduction in the petty arguments between my husband and me. Instead of engaging in back and forth text wars when a petty or careless yet hurtful comment was made, or why he had to drop dirty socks all over the place instead of putting them in the laundry basket (can you relate?), I was able to go beyond all that daily drama, effectively communicate on a whole new level, free up so much energy, and simply enjoy the day more!

The heart has connected differing world religions, philosophies, and spiritual traditions throughout time. The heart is mentioned 878 times in the modern Bible, in 59 out of 73 of its books. We see the prominence of the Heart Sutra in Buddhism and the Sacred Heart of Jesus Christ in Catholicism. In the Islamic Koran the term *qalb*, which translates to "heart," appears 132 times. In the ancient Judaic tradition, the Torah speaks of the "wisdom of the heart," and the notion of *Lev*, which repeatedly refers to the heart in the instructions concerning the Tabernacle. In the Hindu and yogic traditions, the heart is the seat of the *anahata* chakra, which, along with the spiritual eye, is the central point of consciousness and connection to Spirit.

The heart is also seen as more than just a physical organ in spiritual traditions around the world. It is believed to be a gateway to the soul, the True Self, the connection to the larger or higher self, Spirit, or Universal intelligence. Or in other words, *the heart is the central place in which our humanness and Spirit merge.*

Ancient cultures worldwide, including the Babylonians and Greeks, believed that the heart was the primary organ capable of influencing and directing emotions and decision-making. The ancient Egyptians believed that the heart housed thought and the soul. They weighed a person's heart after they passed away to determine the level of truth and justice in their life. A cornerstone of both the centuries-old traditional Chinese medicine and Ayurvedic medicine systems is to take the pulse of the heart, which is used as a key assessment of the body's overall energetic and health state. It's only in modern times that this view has changed, with the central emphasis on the brain as our most important organ.

The wise ancients across the world and centuries knew something that can greatly benefit modern society: that our hearts are a central point of profound power and intelligence. Our hearts are more than we think they are. And they have a lot to teach us.

You don't need to adhere to any specific spiritual beliefs to benefit from the biological insights about the heart in this book or to employ the science-backed techniques for fostering heart intelligence in your life. However, if you are so inclined, these tools can enrich spiritual practices like meditation and prayer. My own experience was that even with years of meditation, accessing heart intelligence further elevated the depth and joy of my practice.

And beyond the times you meditate, learning to harness and utilize your heart's power means you can feel the peace, undistracted presence, love, and kindness not just when you are meditating, but rather when you need it the most: in the middle of your busy, everyday life.

IS THE HEART TRUSTWORTHY?

Maybe you always intuitively sensed the enormous power inside of your heart, but you didn't know how to harness it. Maybe right now you're thinking, *Right on! Show me the way into my heart! I always knew it!* Or maybe going into your heart sounds a bit scary. Like, *Uh oh. I don't know if I can ever trust my heart.* This is probably so if you've equated your heart with erratic, strong emotions and irrational feelings. You might also recall a time when you felt, *My heart really messed things up for me. I fell for this guy, followed my heart, and it was the worst mistake of my life.* You may therefore think the "rational" brain is superior, while your heart is sentimental and untrustworthy.

The opposite is true. The ego, or mind, places its identity in the "little me," or the small self. The little me is the mind's limited and surface way of seeing things, which often makes us feel fragmented (the opposite of wholeness) within ourselves, as if we are broken and in dire need of getting fixed or being "better" than we already are. The ego can't see deeper, and we can't make it see deeper! We must go to a different place to find the solution.

The real problem is not us, but when we start to believe the wild horse mind and all its thoughts, which create limited beliefs. These beliefs might tell you that you don't belong, that you must compete aggressively, or that another's success diminishes your own. It might lead you to constantly compare yourself to others, creating a sense of separation and a divisive lesser than or greater than mindset. To cope, we often develop strong attachments or aversions as protective mechanisms. As in, *I need this person to feel loved and okay; I can't lose this job or I will be doomed!* Or, *If I'm still single in my 40s* (or *still 20 pounds overweight* or *don't make X amount as a salary,* or fill in the blank*), I am for sure a loser.*

Not only are these beliefs baseless, but they can also be harmful to both your health and peace of mind. They give rise to turbulent emotions such as anger, fear, desire, worry, infatuation, jealousy, and frustration. These emotions disrupt the balance within your body, creating chaos in your organs and systems, thus diminishing your quality of life. All these emotions and behaviors stem from the ego, not the heart.

It's time we stop giving away our power. It's time we stop depleting our own health and living a confused, anxious, and average existence. The problem up until this point is that the ego mind has been running the show (your life), unbridled (picture the wild horse trampling on beautiful flowers and breaking fences). The solution is found, you guessed it, in your heart.

Only in awakening your heart can you realize the truth of who you really are, beneath all the limited beliefs of the egoic mind. And experiencing that truth, which is exactly what The Five Hearts will support you with, will change your entire life.

Key Points of Your Brilliant Heart

- Heart brilliance, a high-powered kind of intelligence, refers to an untapped power beyond the heart's biological function, which includes the science of heart coherence, or heart-brain communication, and bringing forward the heart's intuitive wisdom.

- Awakening your heart's brilliant intelligence will transform your physical health, confidence, relationships, and emotional resilience, and greatly expand abundance, success, inner peace, and fulfillment across your life.

- The heart is a kind of brain and contains 40,000 neurons, or brain-like cells. The heart sends more messages to the brain than vice versa.

- The heart is what connects ancient cultures, spiritual traditions, and all major world religions.

In the next chapter, we are going to discuss The Five Hearts, the stages of heart coherence and heart awakening that we all go through on our journey to unlock our heart's power.

Let's continue!

Chapter 2

THE FIVE HEARTS

The way we access our heart's massive power and intelligence happens through five stages, known as The Five Hearts. In each stage, you experience a completely different reality.

As you move through the heart stages, you will progressively be able to create major breakthroughs in your life, such as feeling more at peace with yourself, overcoming stressful thoughts, finding or deepening your relationship with your life partner, realizing quantum leaps of success in your career, and creating harmony within your family. What separates each stage is the degree to which your heart's innate intelligence is unlocked.

YOUR INNER REALITY WILL CHANGE
YOUR OUTER REALITY

While all spiritual traditions contain teachings on the heart, our journey through The Five Heart stages is a modern interpretation inspired by the teachings of Sri Yukteswar.[4] A mystic of penetratingly deep wisdom and profound understanding of ancient Vedic science, Sri Yukteswar laid out guidance around these Five Heart stages to provide us with a vision—a map for understanding our heart's potential—in order to realize the truth of who we really are. These stages also correspond to the science of heart coherence, starting with the first stage, where we experience incoherence, progressively all the way to heart-brain harmony in the last stage.

As we embark on this journey together, it's really important to read The Five Heart stages in chronological order to best understand the heart's journey in its totality. Some stages may feel foreign, which is totally fine. No matter which heart stage you currently resonate with, please explore the teachings and practices within all the stages. Even a single insight, a single realization, can plant a seed within you, leading to profound transformation and personal growth.

Remember, your path to awakening your amazing heart will be completely unique to you. It isn't going to be like anyone else's, and it's not going to be linear. While the mind likes things in a straightforward way, like following an instruction manual for an electronic device, that's just not how the heart operates.

The heart works in its own completely dynamic way. Be prepared for pauses, times when you feel no forward movement, as your heart is working to release an old engrained pattern that is not in alignment with who you really are. For example, you may wake up to seeing your own people-pleasing behavior, how you self-sabotage your own abundant opportunities or love interests because deep down you don't feel that you are worthy or you are trying to exert control, resist intimacy, overrely on food to feel soothed, hold on to resentment, or whatever patterns that keep you back in your life. And yet these behaviors may still play out for a time—until you are ready to follow your heart and finally let them go.

Also know that at any time you may experience quantum leaps, times where in an instant your heart shows you the way to a whole new reality or perspective. And whatever you do, don't compare your journey to another's. There's no need to ever compare. All hearts are equal, and each is on its own path. Trust the process.

You may resonate with one heart stage predominantly, but you may also find yourself oscillating between different stages. This fluidity is totally natural. It's not about regression but about continually shedding more of what's not in alignment with who you really are. There's no rush to progress from one stage to another, and there's no need to try to force your heart open.

For instance, I've spent a lot of my life in the Propelled Heart, which is Stage 2, and I now have many moments and extended periods of experiencing the vast, all-encompassing love in the Devoted Heart, which is Stage 4. And yet, deepening more into the Steady Heart, which is Stage 3 and in between those two stages is currently where my personal work lies. Once again, The Five Hearts are not necessarily linear. Yet I know that the more I expand my Steady Heart, the more I will experience the bliss characteristic of the Devoted and Clear Heart stages.

I've had such a deep past of identifying with my achievements, with labels in general, and with not feeling enough. Ingrained patterns reshape in their own time and way. And so at times I still get unsteady from triggers, especially around these topics. At a recent conference, I couldn't help but compare that more people went to the talk across the hall than mine. Even though my room was fairly full, I still got in my head. I felt a flash of self-doubt, *Does anyone care what I talk about, anyways?* And I was thrown off as I began my talk. I recovered and got back on track after doing the HeartAlign Steady in Life Practice right there on stage (which you will learn about in a later chapter). But there was still in front of me—still *in* me somewhere—comparison and self-judgment. The very qualities of "The Unsteady Heart," if I wrote a chapter called that.

Perhaps the most self-judgment I experienced was during a Dark Heart period, which is Stage 1, after my mom passed. It was sudden (within six weeks of her cancer diagnosis), and life started to feel very unsteady. I worried about what was going to happen to my dad. And it brought other instabilities to the forefront, like the relationship I was in. It was not moving forward, and we were not getting closer. In fact, there was a distance that had been growing for a while that I did not want to acknowledge but eventually could not deny. In the aftermath of my mom's passing, when our baby was around a year and a half old, I moved out. And then I pinned myself in a singular identity, drenched with the deepest of self-judgment: *single mom.* There is nothing wrong with being a single mom, of course! But oh, the stories and the crap I was telling myself about what it meant about me. In my ego mind, I told myself I couldn't hold down a partner or a family. I made it mean that I was a mess and a failure and not worthy of love.

That low point was more than seven years ago now as I tell you about this. In the following chapters, I will also share some stories with you about meeting and connecting with my husband, the love of my life and a living demonstration that abundant love is possible at any point in our lives. I was actually worthy of love all along, like all of us, I just had to realize it. I've expanded my Steady Heart far more. It doesn't mean that I'm not unsteady at times, because as I just mentioned, I still feel those waves of self-doubt that I am working on. But they do come less. *Far* less.

And I come back faster. These very practices that I will share throughout The Five Heart chapters have been life-changing for me, and I hope they will also be for you.

The process of expanding your heart's brilliant intelligence will unfold in its own way too. However, by deepening your awareness of each stage and doing the HeartAlign System practices offered throughout the book, you will greatly support your heart's continued awakening.

The end of each heart stage chapter includes a Heart Embodiment section with practical lifestyle tips to further support your awakening heart. These sections include suggested foods to eat, daily practices, and other tools. You are both form and unseen energy (really all a continuum of energy), and everything is connected, so these holistic lifestyle practices will be enormously helpful in unlocking your heart as well.

Before we go any further, I want to outline The Five Hearts for you and give you a preamble to what we will discuss in the pages that follow.

STAGE 1: THE DARK HEART—INCOHERENCE

This is a stage of disconnection from your heart. It often results in experiencing stress, frustration, fear, great confusion, unawareness, separation from others, overwhelm, negative behaviors or emotions, or perhaps not feeling at all. This stage corresponds to incoherence, a state where the heart and brain are not in communication. This appears in disordered, chaotic heart rhythm patterns.

However lost you feel—as we all do at times—your heart center is still there and can be nurtured back. The Dark Heart is a starting point that prompts moving forward into more self-awareness and growth through challenges. It's also a stage that can be experienced in periods of your life or reverted back to at any period, as more old identifications, delusions, or false ideas come up to be shed.

STAGE 2: THE PROPELLED HEART—THE BEGINNING OF COHERENCE

At this stage, the heart has begun to open, and you can feel access to far more energy. Characterized by seeking meaning and truth in life, it propels you into action, whether that is directed toward getting in better shape, adopting a healthier diet or lifestyle, or moving up in your career. The beginning of coherence emerges, meaning that the heart and the brain are in better communication.

However, at this stage there is a great tendency to overthink, which often drowns out the more subtle, intuitive wisdom of the heart. This leads to restlessness, stress, anxiety, and burnout. Other trappings of this stage include pride and a rigid sense of the "right way," as the search for meaning often gets placed into personal beliefs, ideas, and opinions. A big focus in this stage is to be more resilient against stress from within and to create greater harmony with each moment of life.

STAGE 3: THE STEADY HEART— COHERENCE AND CONNECTION

This is the first stage where the heart starts to lead your life instead of the ego, and this creates a sense of inner stability and connection to your center within. The realization that you can be steady grows, no matter what is going on outside of you; and your thoughts, feelings, and physical sensations don't have to become your identity. You begin to let go of attachments and trying to control life.

You discover more resilience against life's challenges, and that the circumstances in your life seem to flow better when *you* are in your center. You experience greater awareness as more harmony, or *entrainment,* with the heart, brain, and nervous system is created. A major focus in this stage is creating emotional intelligence, which is rooted in heart intelligence and increases abundance and success across all areas of your life.

STAGE 4: THE DEVOTED HEART—
INTUITION AND FORGIVENESS

This is a high stage of heart awakening, a place of great rising peace and joy that becomes unlocked. You become more devoted, and more in tune with the inner world than the fluctuating outer world. Intuition, or direct knowing or perception, rises because the inner connection to the heart is so strong. This high heart intelligence and high coherence open the door to expansive solutions not previously available.

The extraordinary power of unconditional love and the other heart qualities of peace, compassion, appreciation, and care come forward as the dominant energies of your life. Service for others, by simply bringing the presence of more peace and love forward into the world, becomes primary. The restless thoughts of the mind are largely dissolved by the heart's expanding intelligence, coherence, and the alignment of heart-brain power. You keep experiencing more abundance across your life as you continue to shed, forgive, and let go of what is not of the heart.

STAGE 5: THE CLEAR HEART—
HEART-BRAIN HARMONY

This is a stage of unity, deep connection to oneself and others, and imperturbable inner peace. The heart and brain become one, melding into the highest level of heart-brain harmony and a seamless integration of heart intelligence and brain function. The highest heart qualities flow through transparently, fully and constantly, including compassion, peace, care, appreciation, love, and bliss. This stage enables the highest levels of creativity, innovation, and intuitive knowing as well as great synchronicities and the seemingly miraculous.

A NEW, HEART-CENTERED SOCIETY

The Five Hearts apply to each of us as individuals as well as to the collective as a whole. Opening your heart and awakening your heart's power isn't just about your individual gain. You will most definitely benefit tremendously in your life as you tap into the teachings and practices in this book to awaken your heart; though beyond that, we must recognize that we're all part of an intricately connected larger whole.

The more hearts that awaken into heart intelligence, the more a new society will be shaped and formed. A more heart-awakened society that operates in greater harmony, unity, kindness, and compassion, and with more love and appreciation for ourselves and each other. Divisiveness and separation transform into acceptance and collaboration. It sounds idealistic, and it surely is. But it's also possible, one heart at a time.

We know what it looks like when much of society is in the Dark Heart. What would it look like if society entered a new heart stage with more heart intelligence within each person, and with each other?

Each of us can be—and can spread—a heart-based movement of more unity, acceptance, and harmony across society.

As you awaken your heart and tap into your heart intelligence, you will change your life and open up a channel to help others do the same. It starts with creating more heart-based living within your home and family life, and in your inner circles that include your children, friends, neighbors, and colleagues, and flowing out from there. By awakening your own heart, you will affect countless others. Paramahansa Yogananda said, "Reform yourself and you will reform thousands."[5]

There is a new time rising. A time of heart awakening that will transform everything. You're a part of it. I'm a part of it. We're all a part of it.

Let's start the journey of a lifetime. The journey to find the center of you. The journey into your own incredible heart.

Key Points of The Five Hearts

- There are Five Heart stages to unlock in order to fully awaken your heart's brilliance.

- These stages are inspired by the work of the great yoga mystic Sri Yukteswar, and each stage corresponds to the science of heart coherence (from incoherence to heart-brain harmony).

- The more we awaken our hearts, the more we can change our lives and contribute to a more heart-based society, starting with the circles around us.

Now that we have laid a foundational understanding of heart intelligence and the Five Heart stages, we are ready to dive deeper.

Let's now explore the first stage, The Dark Heart.

Chapter 3

STAGE 1

THE DARK HEART: INCOHERENCE

Darkness sounds, well, dark. And perhaps a bit sinister. However, I'm not referring to dark as in *bad*. I mean the kind of dark where you can't see clearly. Think about trying to walk across a dark room. You may stumble into a table, bang your knee really hard against a cabinet (ouch), and knock over a few vases and lamps. It's not your fault that you made a mess per se—you can't see where you're going!

When we're in the Dark Heart stage, we're cut off from our hearts and can't see ourselves—or life—clearly. Such periods can span moments, days, weeks, or even longer. Confusion and frustration often arise because it's the ego, the unbridled and overthinking mind (that wild, untamed horse!), instead of the heart, leading your life. Sri Yukteswar says of this stage, "In the dark state of the heart, man harbors misconceptions (about everything)."[6]

This means incoherence, which means that mostly your head is talking rather than the heart and brain communicating *together.* This can make you feel locked in dark thoughts and heavy emotions like self-doubt, fear, anger, blame, and frustration. And without the vital connection to the heart's light, you may start to believe the dark thoughts, such as you are not good enough. These harsh thoughts are completely untrue. But they can certainly feel like they are when we're in this stage.

It can feel forced or inauthentic to make yourself feel positive when you simply don't. And that's why many motivational programs sound great but don't work out so well in the long term. Trying to just think positive thoughts doesn't get to the root of the disconnection. An internal shift from the ego to the heart leading our life is required so that we can bring light to the darkness. Once we understand this, we can work on making this shift, starting today.

RECONNECTING TO THE HEART AND GROWTH THROUGH CHALLENGES

I've gone through many Dark Heart stages in my life, like most of us. These have included drinking my way through college to the point of blacking out many times— going into literal darkness. At its root, I did this to mask and pacify the massive anxiety and insecurities I was feeling. There were also dark times of bulimia in high school, throwing up because I was so disconnected from myself and my feelings, and I couldn't "digest" life.

There was darkness when my mom passed away suddenly, and I felt like I couldn't trust life. And as I mentioned earlier, I went into a Dark Heart stage when I became a single mom for a time. It wasn't the life that I imagined or wanted, and I feared that I might be on my own forever. I've encountered "dark nights of the soul," of feeling deep confusion and inner turmoil, even when my life looked great from the outside.

As you read this, some of your own dark times may come to mind. Times when you felt frustrated with life or simply felt low. Maybe your heavy mindset was reflected in extra weight in your body. Maybe you felt burdened by the heaviness of life's responsibilities, caring for children and aging parents, or trying to find a job you actually like while struggling to pay the bills. Maybe you felt darkness and a lot of confusion, but you didn't want to tell anyone about it, so you put on a happy face.

Remember, no matter how lost or lonely you may feel, the power of your heart remains, ever-present and waiting to come forward in your life. This book offers you tools to help you reconnect with this innate power. (If you ever find yourself deeply struggling, it's essential to also seek professional counseling and support.)

Slowly but surely, you will learn to start centering yourself in the light of your own heart. It's not in pushing away darkness that we dispel it, but by bringing in the light. Paramahansa Yogananda said, "Bring the light in and you will feel that darkness never was."[7]

DARKNESS IS A GREAT TEACHER

Moving through each Dark Heart period can lead to incredible growth. I know this to be true in my own life. The potential of the Dark Heart is to be a great teacher, showing us how to return to our center in order to live life from the place of feeling whole, the truth of who we really are. We can either move through the challenges and open our hearts further, or we can remain in darkness longer. And our hearts will wait until we are ready.

Sri Yukteswar says of when we are in the Dark Heart, "He can grasp only ideas of the physical world."[8] We run into trouble if we believe that only what we can see with our physical eyes is real. That's a big no-no. Why? Because then we might look at our current bank account or living circumstances and believe that life is indeed hard, that maybe we should just give up.

But actually, all that we see with our physical eyes was created in the past. To move forward, to get out of the dark, we must start connecting to the energy inside of us. The energy that we embody now creates our life in the future.

Imagine you fell in love with the most amazing puppy from the pound who just made you feel over the moon with love every time you saw him. You wouldn't care one bit that he had a limp paw and were slightly cross-eyed and missing part of an ear, would you? Why? Because you went beyond the physical to feel the connection on a deeper level. You don't see lack in that puppy. You only see love. This is exactly what you need to do across your life. If your life right now kind of feels like a limp puppy, you must start connecting to the power and energy that is right here, right now in you below the surface!

While we can't see our heart intelligence with our physical eyes, we can tap into it. So how do we do that? We must go beyond the linear mind, beyond letting the wild horse mind run the show, and decide *I've had enough of this!* Instead, you move into a much deeper place. That place is your heart, which is where you can access your True Self. It's actually quite simple to do. As you shift to your heart, you walk through a doorway to a deeper place of existence and understanding, and you transcend the choppy surface of life.

The great thing about our work in this book to unlock your heart's power is that you don't have to trust me or take my word for it. You're going to start *experiencing* it for yourself. And as you learn to move beyond the physical world and open your heart *first*, your physical world will transform. That's how it works.

Foundational Practice: Heart Shift

You may have lost touch with your heart, with your center, and therefore felt lost to who you really are. While someone can survive in a brain-dead state, as in a coma or with life support, no one can survive without a heart. *There is no life without your heart.* That is true physically, but many still move through life disconnected from their heart, so they are not alive, emotionally or energetically. This cutting off of heart intelligence can create a major blockage across your life that also blocks you from ever feeling truly alive and joyful.

It's time to get back in touch with your power center, which is your amazing heart, or in deeper touch with it— whatever the case may be for you. Remember: no matter how disconnected you may feel from your heart at the moment, the connection can be rekindled.

As you start intentionally shifting to your heart and getting out of your head, which is what we are going to start doing in this practice, you will see how differently you feel in your body and in your perceptions. Research published by Rollin McCraty, PhD. of the HeartMath Institute and his colleagues at the *American Journal of Cardiology* found that by simply shifting your awareness to your heart, you enhance communication between your heart and your brain,[9] help bring your nervous system back into balance, heighten cardiovascular efficiency, and bring more coherence to your emotions and mind.[10]

Can you start to see how powerful and *simple* this is? All this amazing power is right inside your own heart. It's a choice that you make, and you make that choice by shifting your focus over and over again to your heart. We'll build on this heart shift in the other HeartAlign practices you're going to learn throughout the book.

Let's begin to reconnect with these three steps:

1. **Shift your full awareness to your heart.** With eyes closed, shift your full focus and attention right into your heart center. You can bring your hands over your heart if it helps you do that. Start to connect with your amazing heart. Simply by placing your intentional focus and awareness on your heart, you activate its power and vast intelligence to begin waking up in your life, right in this very moment.

2. **Stay in this position for one minute (or more).**

3. **Create an awareness of what you intuitively feel and sense.** Take note of what happens when you shift your awareness to your heart. Do you feel calmer, more expansive, that you are slowing down? Do any emotions come up for you?

Ultimately there are no right or wrong answers here. This practice is about reconnecting you with the center of your incredible heart and revitalizing this all-important connection. There is so much latent wisdom and power in there. It sounds incredible because it really is! Can you start to connect to it? Maybe or maybe not yet, and either way it's okay. It's a process, and you only have to let yourself take the journey and keep tuning inward.

You can return to this practice at any time, even when sitting at your desk in the middle of a busy workday or on the edge of your tub after you shower, to check in and create more awareness about yourself and your heart in the present moment.

THE POWER OF HEART COHERENCE

Imagine talking to a friend where there is a natural, harmonious vibe to the conversation, and you feel simultaneously relaxed, energized, and inspired from the exchange. Compare this to a tense conversation, where you and the other person are constantly interrupting and talking over each other. You feel angry and annoyed and don't even make eye contact or listen to each other. The first kind of amazing, in-sync conversation is coherence, and the two friends are—you guessed it—your heart and your brain. They really can be great allies once they start talking to each other. The second conversation is an incoherent conversation. And we all know that being in those frustrating conversations feels horrible.

Coherence is the synchronization or the syncing up of systems within your body. You become like a finely tuned machine where everything is working at its the best. Coherence *has* to start with your heart, since it's the strongest biological oscillator, or rhythm setter, in the body.

When you activate your heart's power, it creates more aligned communication between your heart, brain, and nervous system, and then facilitates better communication with the rest of the body. *With your brain and heart in sync, your overall health and bodily efficiency improve significantly.*

Imagine swimming to the opposite shore of a river in one straight, smooth swim. Compare that to what it feels like energetically if, on the same swim, you hit a big rock you have to maneuver around, you pause and tread water to clear out water from your goggles twice, and you backtrack several times because you swam in the wrong direction completely.

Heart coherence is like the smooth, flowing swim across, which is efficient and clear. Incoherence is like that inefficient latter swim where so much energy is wasted. The more coherent you become, starting with your heart and flowing out, the more energy you have to maintain your physical health—you have more vitality and you put less strain on your organs. All systems, including your digestive and immune systems, function better.

Coherence is a core part of accessing your heart intelligence, and it can be measured physically, as shown by smooth, rhythmic patterns in your heart rate variability. (If you're interested, you can measure and learn how to increase your heart coherence in real time with a heart coherence app and sensor. See the Resources section.) When you feel coherent, you feel calm, clear, focused, intuitive, energized, and in sync with yourself and the world around you. You can see in the following graphs that when you are in the incoherent emotion of anger, your heart rhythms (HRV pattern) are chaotic and disordered. This chaos is then unfortunately carried through all the systems of your body.

On the other hand, when you are in coherent, calm emotions like appreciation and care, your heart's rhythms are smooth and orderly. And this is also echoed through the body in a smooth, orderly flow.

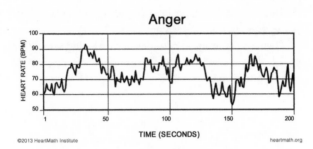

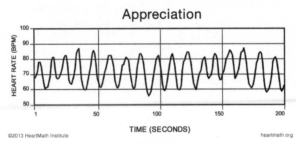

Changes in heart rhythm patterns before and after engaging in coherence, using tools to self-generate positive emotions (in this case, appreciation). Measured by subjects in HeartMath research studies. (Courtesy of the HeartMath Institute, 2024.)

Heart Coherence

Heart coherence is when your heart pattern is rhythmic, smooth, and efficient. Coherence then creates smooth and efficient communication to your brain.

To perform at your best and continually make the best day-to-day decisions, your heart and brain must be in harmony with one another.

The rest of your body's systems, including your nervous system, become more efficient.

This results in maximum energy and efficiency, clarity, lighter thoughts, and feeling more connection to yourself and others.

Activating Heart Intelligence through Heart Coherence + Managing your mind + Managing your emotions	=	Energy efficiency Greater physical health Enhanced awareness Greater productivity More mental clarity, calmness, and peace Higher access to intuition Access to heart emotions at will (appreciation, love, compassion, and joy)

HEART COHERENCE IS THE ROOT OF CALM, COMMON SENSE, AND POSITIVE THINKING

Coherence, however, is about so much more than your physical body's benefits (as enormous as those are!). Coherence is a state of being. As you become more in sync within your body through the practices in this book, you become more in sync with the world around you. This means you're able to make better decisions and have more awareness. You start to see more, in the way of deeper understanding.

It's as if the lights in the dark room are turning on, one at a time. The more coherent we become, sustaining it for longer periods and more often, the more lights that get turned on. Because everything in your life is created from the inside out, this inner harmony will then flow out from your body and into more harmony and success across your whole life. This also means that in your current job or relationships, you will be able to see more! This could mean you get some new, big ideas to create a project at work that is completely different from anything you've ever done. Or within your relationship with your mother-in-law or your mother or colleague, you suddenly see where they are coming from and feel far more connected rather than separated from them. It's like taking off a blindfold you didn't realize you were wearing!

Heart coherence will help you create more peace and joy in your life, and that means something very important: staying right here in this moment. Whether we realize it or not, past events and old emotional memories are recognized in the amygdala part of your brain and can bring pain and fear from the past into the present. This leads to reactivity, energy-draining overthinking, and the tendency to make things mean so much!

Over time, the heart will more easily be able to lasso the mind into more clarity, coherence, and focus. Your thoughts will become lighter and more positive. The patterns of your brain and heart cell communication can rewire, known as *neuroplasticity* (this is typically thought of just in terms of brain cells but also applies to heart-brain communication as there are 40,000 neurons in the heart).

Coherence in daily life looks like:

- Having connected, inspired conversations throughout the day

- Expressing your needs and having them met

- Simply and effortlessly choosing the best foods to eat based on what feels right for your body in that moment, without overthinking or overanalyzing

- Finding harmony with all those around you

- Having lighter thoughts, and feeling lighter and more peaceful

Coherence is like looking through a clear lake to see each rock on the sandy bottom. On the other hand, when you're incoherent, it's like not seeing a thing through choppy waves. When you're physically and mentally coherent, it opens the door for your intuition to flow. And incredible, even brilliant, solutions suddenly pop into your awareness that could not be accessed in states of incoherence.

Say, for example, you're in line at the coffee shop and someone comes in and pushes in front of you in line. Something about their pushy behavior sets you off. Even though you may not consciously register it, that present-moment experience may have correlated to an old memory, stored deep in your brain, of getting cut in line by an older bully back in grade school. Subconsciously, your amygdala starts triggering you faster than you can even understand.[11] Because it's all happening so fast, it can keep you locked into automated reactions. Suddenly, you're seething with anger as you stand there in line. You feel personally violated. *How dare that jerk do that to me!* You silently fume. You're stuck in the Dark Heart's incoherence.

Your heart's racing, and you're shaking slightly. Identifying with these lower vibration, victim-type thoughts moves your heart rhythms into an erratic pattern and warps your communication with your nervous system. Your body is now in a fight-or-flight stress response state. There is also additional stress placed on your organs, and your digestive, immune, and hormonal systems have all been compromised. Geez. All of this from one incident.

Applying your heart intelligence and creating more heart coherence in the moment can look like this: You become aware that you are starting to become triggered. You notice your heart rate speeding up and your thoughts racing. You immediately shift your focus into your heart, take some deep, coherence-building breaths. You practice the HeartAlign Harmonize Method. This helps you create coherence and access your heart intelligence on the spot in real life, in mere seconds, which you will learn about in the Propelled Heart stage.

This tool will help you regulate your thoughts back into peaceful rhythms, right in the moment. *It's no big deal,* you tell yourself. *Maybe he's in a huge rush. I hope he gets all that he needs to get done. It will probably only take about three more minutes in line. I will send that e-mail from my phone that I have to send anyway.*

As you can see, this is about your heart and your brain working together. Turning this chaotic situation around, which was all taking place internally, would feel like a huge battle from the mind alone. Mentally, it would take an enormous amount of energy to try to overpower these dark thoughts. Instead, the heart got turned on *first.* Your heart has infinite power to shift things around for you in each present moment of life. Once you begin to turn on your heart intelligence, it will direct you toward calm and common-sense thinking. The more you do this, the more your life will change. It starts with the micromoments.

THE ULTIMATE ENERGY BOOSTER

Hold on, though; the micromoments and shifts turn out not to be so micro! Even seemingly small episodes of anger, annoyance, and stress can throw off your body for *hours.*

For example, the following graph shows research from Rollin McCraty and his team from the HeartMath Institute, who found that just *five minutes of anger impaired the immune system for at least six hours!* In this study they measured levels of *IgA,* an important secretory antibody that increases immunity, making you more resistant to infection and disease. The researchers found levels of IgA were increased by emotions of care and decreased by the emotion of anger. And this is not to mention the other systems in your body, which are pretty much all thrown into chaos from these incoherent thoughts. Clearly, it takes a long time for your system to rebound from erratic and unbridled emotions!

You can also see that activating coherent thoughts boosted immunity in measurable ways. This awareness is important so that you can start to move out of the incoherent, old, rigid ways that brought so much heaviness to your life into new ways that feel light and free.

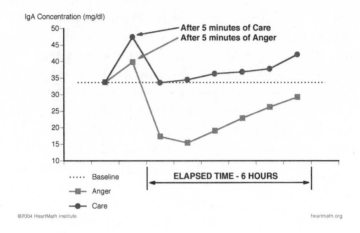

Testing the effects of various emotions on IgA, an important secretory antibody that increases immunity, making you more resistant to infection and disease. When participants were asked to recall an experience of anger for five minutes, their IgA levels spiked and then dropped to half of what they were before the anger, and even after six hours, had not returned to normal.[12] In contrast, when study participants were asked to invoke feelings of care and compassion for five minutes, their IgA levels also immediately increased and then continued to steadily increase over six hours. (Courtesy of the HeartMath Institute.)

OPENING THE ENERGETIC HEART

Heart coherence also opens the door to awakening the energetic or spiritual heart. This is because as your physical heart calms into an ordered, smooth pattern, you become calmer. And calmness is absolutely essential for your energetic heart to come online and awaken more powerfully in your life.

Sri Yukteswar says that the delusions, or maya, "makes him forget his real Self and brings about all his sufferings."[13]

Delusions occur when we are too caught up in the little dramas of daily life, giving them too much of our time and attention. Then we can become stuck in incoherent thoughts like *He said this* and *He should have said that*, or *This is the worst* (whatever *this* happens to be at that particular moment), or *My coffee tasted horrible today* (maybe so, but you are still complaining about it three hours later!). And we remain in the limited existence of the Dark Heart. When we get entangled in the dramas of life, no matter how important they may seem in that moment, we're in the ego and not in our hearts. And so our hearts' power gets cut off.

In darkness, you can't see across the table or into the mirror correctly, right? Yet as coherence grows, so will more of your true vision, which creates more light to see in your life. Research shows that as you become more coherent you will experience more positive perceptions.[14] Of course, people may say or do mean things and disruptions in life can still occur. From your intelligent heart's perspective though, guess what? *You simply move on.* It's not such a big deal anymore.

Your awakening heart is the doorway to allowing more of the heart intelligent emotions—care, compassion, joy, peace, love, and appreciation—to flow into your life and recharge you and the ideas of the ego or false self, which focus on lack and victim mentality, to drop away.

With more light starting to pour in, bit by bit, you recognize that life isn't so heavy and dark after all. And wow, you aren't really a terrible person. Sure, you had some missteps, but you were doing the best you could at the time with where you were. And you realize for yourself the great truth: You don't have to fix yourself but rather be more of yourself. *It was the insecure thoughts that were the problem all along, not you.*

A PERSONAL NOTE

After many years of practicing meditation, I am so excited to share the HeartAlign Meditation with you, which combines the best of science and ancient wisdom. In my daily meditations, I would often find stillness and get to some energetically expansive places. But once I got up and the day would set in, so would some—or at times a lot of—incoherence. Sometimes my wild horse mind would take me to old reactions or negative or low thoughts, and calm and peace were nowhere to be found.

This meditation dropped me into my heart and I felt a centering power in my daily life I had never before been able to access. A rising peace and clarity made the solutions now obvious to all these little and larger questions I used to have. I feel more connected to myself and in all my relationships. I'm so excited for you to experience amazing benefits too!

This in no way takes away from the deepest of yogic meditation practices, such as the Kriya Yoga method taught by Paramahansa Yogananda. Kriya Yoga has been passed down for millennia from ancient India and is the core of Raja Yoga, the royal or highest path of yoga, which I also personally practice. If you feel called to go deeper into definite scientific techniques of meditation and pranayama yogic science, please also follow that calling (see the Resources section for more information on this).

The HeartAlign Meditation

The HeartAlign Meditation has been proven to efficiently increase your coherence and clarity,[15] tap into your heart intelligence, and open your energetic heart. I have adapted the HeartAlign Meditation from HeartMath's Quick Coherence Technique, with their permission, and also incorporated some of Yogananda's techniques.

The more you practice this meditation, the more you will feel inner harmony, peace, and clarity rising up from your heart and out into your day and life. Coherence will continue to build, day by day. And the other great news? *This meditation can be practiced in under 10 minutes!*

The team at my company, Solluna, ran a study on the HeartAlign Meditation with the HeartMath Institute's research team. Thirty participants practiced the meditation over four weeks, four to five times a week.[16] There was an *average increase of 29 percent in coherence* levels of participants being able to shift into and sustain a state of coherence. And importantly, there was a 10 percent increase in their resting state coherence levels, indicating that they had established a new baseline of coherence (no matter what they happened to be doing). In other words, the participants had reprogrammed their nervous systems to a more optimal functional state in just one month.

Aim to practice this meditation four to five times a week like the study participants to glean the maximum coherence benefits (you can do it if you commit to it!). Anytime you are able to practice, it however, you will build your coherence capacity. I recommend doing the meditation in the morning, as close as possible to waking. The HeartAlign Meditation will help you access your heart intelligence first thing and will increasingly impact your whole day from the morning up (which is how I teach making lifestyle changes too, by the way).

You can also practice this meditation in the evenings to help you reset to a state of greater harmony, for deeper, more peaceful rest. You can also work it into the middle of your day to increase coherence and prevent misconceptions, confusion, and tension from building in the busyness of daily life.

There are complimentary tracks of this meditation on my site, paired with music. If you'd like to practice together, I would love to guide you through (please see the Resources section)! The steps of the HeartAlign Meditation are as follows:

1. Tense your whole body as you inhale and then relax your body with a double exhale. Repeat three times.

2. Shift your awareness to your heart.

3. Keep focusing on your heart while taking five to eight slow breaths in and out, imagining you are breathing from your heart.

4. Self-generate the core heart feeling of appreciation, which means recalling a person or event to help you tap into this expansive feeling.

5. Sustain your heart focus and appreciation for three to four minutes or more.

6. Close with a moment of thanking your heart's wisdom and setting an intention to stay connected to it as you move forward into your day.

A more detailed explanation of each step follows:

1. **Tense your whole body as you inhale and then relax your body with a double exhale. Repeat three times.** Close your eyes and inhale as you consciously tense your shoulders, fists, face, and leg muscles to strong tension for a count of three, then release the tension with a big double exhale out of your mouth (making a sound like *huh huhhhh*). Repeat three times. This is based on a method taught by Paramahansa Yogananda. This technique helps to remove the buildup of restless energy, tightness, and tension from your body so you can create more stillness and heart coherence.

2. **Shift your awareness to your heart.** As indicated in the first practice earlier in this chapter, this is the most important shift you can make: from the thoughts, born of your ego and mind, into your

heart. This is hugely important, because you are shifting to another place entirely, rather than trying to overpower "bad" thoughts with "good" thoughts. Shifting your focus and awareness to your heart will also help to create coherence throughout your entire body and calm your nervous system.[17]

3. **Keep focusing on your heart while taking five to eight slow breaths in and out and imagining you are breathing from your heart.** Start taking some deep, full breaths, imagining you are breathing in and out of your heart and maintaining your full focus on your heart. Your conscious breathing will help you connect even more deeply to your heart.

   You can start off by breathing to a count of five breaths in, five breaths out, which translates to a ten-second rhythm, or six breaths per minute. This was the rhythm found in research by HeartMath (measured at 0.1 Hz, a measurement of frequency), to increase heart coherence and shift you into a more coherent state.[18]

   However, it can feel stressful to keep forcing yourself into a set rhythm. After three or so breath cycles, you can simply *relax* into your body's own natural, slow pattern while still focusing on your heart.

4. **Self-generate the core heart feeling of appreciation.** Appreciation is a heart-based and heart-opening energy. It feels expansive because it expands you out beyond the little me—the ego— and connects you to intelligent energy that runs through your heart and all of life. Appreciation is a blend of gratitude, thankfulness, approval, and admiration.[19]

   Self-generating means that while keeping your focus on your heart, recall something that makes you tap into the *feeling* of appreciation. It could be a favorite place in nature, being with a loved one, or a specific event. Then you can release the visual of the person and event and focus on the feeling.

Self-generating a core heart feeling, such as appreciation, was found in the HeartMath Institute's research to help sync up heart and brain communication; increase coherence; regenerate the hormonal, immune, and nervous system; and also facilitate health and well-being. [20][21][22][23][24]

5.   **Sustain your heart focus and appreciation for three to four minutes or more.** Use your will and your sincere intention to maintain focus on your heart while sustaining the powerful energy of appreciation for a few minutes. Staying in this entrained, regulated state creates more heart coherence, which results in deeper coherence within your own bodily systems—on a mental, emotional, spiritual, electromagnetic, and cellular level. It may feel tingly, "warm," or expansive. You may also naturally shift into other core heart emotions: love, joy, peace, or care.

     You will also start to awaken your all-powerful connection to the energetic heart, which will bring you into contact with your personal connection to Spirit.

6.   **Close with a moment of thanking your heart's wisdom and setting an intention to stay connected to it as you move forward into your day.** Doing this meditation shifts you into your heart and activates its all-powerful wisdom. Keep this channel open in your life to continue to create greater coherence, clarity, and creativity as you close out the meditation and move into the rest of your day.

Practiced regularly, the HeartAlign Meditation can shift you from incoherence to coherence and transcend the Dark Heart to experience more lightness, health, happiness, and peace. Again, after only four weeks, study participants increased their baseline coherence 10 percent!

Over time, these steps will flow in the same way as how you brush your teeth. You don't think, *Okay, now it's time to open the cap and put the toothpaste on the toothbrush*—you just do it! And the same will happen here the more you practice it.

Remember that you can check my website for complimentary guided audio tracks of HeartAlign Meditations if you feel that would be helpful for you (see the Resources section).

The following are a few personal experiences of those practicing the HeartAlign Meditation:

- Kappa, a busy, working mother in our Solluna community, related to me that she was feeling frazzled and often overwhelmed with the many demands of everyday life. She had tried meditation before, but her mind raced and she needed more tools to help her deal with the impatience and irritation that often erupted during her busy days. I was so excited to share the HeartAlign Meditation with her. Here's what she reported back:

  After four days of doing the HeartAlign Meditation, my kids were doing something that would normally drive me bananas and have me seeing red. But this time, that angry feeling felt like a distant echo. It was still present, but it was hard to connect to, as if I were observing it rather than truly feeling it. I was able to communicate with my kids from a much calmer and more grounded place.

  Of course, I still have my human moments, but they are becoming fewer than before. Because of feeling appreciation during the meditation, I'm also training myself to find small moments to appreciate, further supporting appreciative feelings throughout my day.

  — Kappa, mother of two

- I met Charles through the wellness and podcast world. I noticed he was really kind but also seemed "inflamed," both physically and in his life. His complexion was slightly ruddy, and he spoke quickly and seemed to have a lot of unexpressed emotions seething under the surface. I shared the HeartAlign Meditation with him, which he also started practicing regularly with his wife. Here's what he shared with me:

  I was in active duty for the military service for six years, and I learned to keep my feelings and head down and plow forward to get things accomplished in a practical way. Many negative thoughts would creep in, though, as well as stress and self-doubt. I tried but never adopted or stuck to a meditation method—until now! When I learned the HeartAlign Meditation, the experience was nothing short of transformational.

  I practice the meditation four to five times a week. And now, not only do I feel a greater dominion over my thoughts, which would often cloud my day, but my emotions now feel more balanced throughout the whole day. I also feel significantly more calm in responding to my daily life's stressors, which include juggling many clients' demands and a very busy schedule. All from an eight-minute meditation. It blows my mind!

  — Charles DeWall, entrepreneur

- Callie, as we will call her, was in major films, often in the press, and placed front and center on magazine covers. When I met her, I could feel how "tight" she was—she was very much in her mind, with lots of thoughts and fears running all the time. She experienced chronic constipation and tightness in her body as well as major insomnia and anxiety. Along with a lifestyle program, including fiber-filled foods and digestion-focused supplements, I introduced her to the HeartAlign

Meditation. We would practice it together over Zoom, and she would also practice with the guided tracks on her own, which she saved on her phone. I could see her whole energy soften and calm before my eyes pre- and postmeditation! It was truly beautiful to see. Here's what she shared:

It's been really hard for me to relax, and this (HeartAlign) meditation helps me do just that. I'm always "on." I always feel stressed. Meditation has always felt so hard, but this one is different. I come in and out of my heart still, but Kimberly's voice always helps me get back in. My day is different when I actually do this! I feel more clear and calm, and I am grateful.

— Callie, actress

THE HEART'S ELECTROMAGNETIC FIELD

There's something amazing happening right from your heart at this very moment: Your heart is generating a significant electromagnetic field. This is essentially a field made of electric and magnetic forces that you can't see with your eyes. Back to what Sri Yukteswar taught us, which is that in order to overcome the misconceptions of the Dark Heart, we have to begin to acknowledge—and start to understand—that there is so much more than what we can see with our physical eyes!

This field is the most powerful one the body produces, dwarfing that of the brain by approximately 100 times in strength.[25] Sensitive instruments, like magnetometers, can detect this field from 8 to 10 feet away from your body.

Your heart field is made of different frequencies that literally create a pattern of light. And this field changes depending on your emotional state.

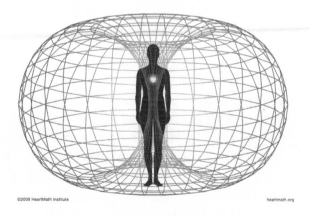

©2009 HeartMath Institute   heartmath.org

The heart's magnetic field. (Courtesy of the HeartMath Institute.)

If you are currently in the Dark Heart stage, it simply means that there is a temporary block to the flow of the light, or electromagnetic frequency, your heart gives off. The incoherence of the Dark Heart causes you to experience overwhelm, fear, confusion, disconnection, frustration, and imbalance, which influences your heart's electromagnetic field.

Your light is still always there, but it is being impeded. This is because you don't feel connected to your heart's power and so others can't feel it either. This diminishes your magnetism, your natural ability to draw people and situations toward you. You also feel disconnected from the energetic heart, which connects us all into the greater field of higher intelligence that we are all part of. Without this essential connection, we feel disconnected and limited across our lives.

Don't worry, because the good news is that you can start to tap into your heart's brilliant light at any time, and your field will accordingly become a stronger frequency as you do! As you learn to create more heart coherence, including by simply shifting into your heart more and by practicing the HeartAlign Meditation at least several times a week, your field will become stronger and feel harmonious.

Just as our emotions and mindset can impact our physical well-being, they influence this powerful heart field, underscoring the interconnectedness of our emotional and physiological states. We are both energy and physical matter (really still energy but more dense!), and the more we live our lives with that important awareness, the more we can make profound changes.

The research also indicates that the energetic information contained in the heart field can be registered by the people around us.[26] This provides scientific evidence to when you feel something intuitively about the mood or the overall "vibe" of someone who walks into the room. Guess what? They can also feel yours!

Start to sense the field others give off around you. I can immediately feel when someone has "great energy," and I just love to be around them. It feels easy and light. Now I know this is because they are in a state of more coherence. For me this includes certain friends that I always look forward to hanging out with, my father, my husband, my son's teacher, and even in the tiny interactions with certain warm, smiling checkout clerks at my favorite little market. Who are some of those people in your life?

On the other hand, before I had the vocabulary of incoherence, whenever I would sense someone felt "off" or all over the place and not really present, I would often label it as "chaotic energy." I used to feel repelled and separate from that person, to varying extents. Sometimes I would make little judgments in my head, and sometimes I would feel the need to go outside of myself and tell my husband or someone close to me that I had an encounter that day that didn't feel so great.

Now, when I am around someone who happens to be in a moment of incoherent, or Dark Heart energy, I know the most powerful thing to do is to go in, not out. What I mean by that is I intentionally come into my heart even more, getting *myself* even more coherent. My coherence often makes *them* more coherent! Then it's easier to connect, and our interaction becomes far more rich, fulfilling, and meaningful.

It doesn't mean I am drawn to seeking that person out to be best friends, but if they are right in front of me, it *is* possible to forge a heart connection in some way. And that feels good. We all move in and out of incoherence at times, so there's no reason to judge. You will also become increasingly coherent with the tools in this book, and then have the stronger vibration in the interaction and the power to shift the energy of that exchange into more connection instead of feeling separation. This is a key way to amplify your abundance, which is about being tapped into the whole. Abundance is the fullness of life, of all things, such as love, material success and opportunities, health, vitality, energy, and more.

Abundance and success will begin to come to you as your heart awakens and your energy field shifts. This is because everyone's personal field has a certain magnetic resonance. Just as magnets attract, as your field's light becomes a stronger, more harmonious frequency, people tend to be more drawn to you, and good things happen.

If you've been looking to create better relationships, find a partner, or access more exciting opportunities at work, and have experienced frustration in these areas, creating greater coherence in your field can help you attract these very things. And at the same time, as your coherence increases, it means you will also experience more inner alignment and peacefulness. While much in life is not in your control, such as the state of the economy or the weather, the great news is that your heart field is in your control.

As you move into more coherence and increasingly out of the incoherence of the Dark Heart, how you feel in your life and what your life looks like have the potential to massively shift and improve.

Practice: Draw Your Own Heart

Take out a notebook or a piece of paper and draw a picture of your heart. Use your intuition rather than thinking too much about it or trying to draw it too literally. It's meant to be symbolic and representative.

What does the field look like around your heart? How much light is shining out of your heart? Are there dark areas? Is the light quite dim right now? Is the whole heart dark in general?

Don't judge or feel bad about yourself, no matter where you currently assess that you are. The point here is to create an awareness, based on your own intuitive wisdom. The more aware you are, the more you can shift, grow, and unblock your heart into its true expansion.

THE IMPORTANCE OF WHO YOU SURROUND YOURSELF WITH

Transcending the Dark Heart is not only about your heart but also about the energy of the hearts that are around you. Paramahansa Yogananda said, "The greatest influence in your life, stronger even than your willpower, is your environment."[27] A big part of your environment is who you spend time with. You've probably felt the impact of who you surround yourself with intuitively, for better or worse.

This makes sense now, when you see that you sense the electromagnetic field others give off, which potentially affects you. Since we want to create more coherence and transcend the Dark Heart stage, carefully choosing who you spend time with is particularly important. It's best to limit time around people who are unhappy in their lives or who are always complaining.

Ask yourself, *How do I feel after being with this person*? The light, the field, or the energy others give off can definitely be felt. Intuitively tune in to the energy inside of your body while being with someone and after spending time with them. Does it feel uplifting? Or depleting?

Trust your heart's guidance here. If someone feels exhausting and takes a lot of your energy to be around, then avoid spending time with them. If that person asks you what's going on, you can answer honestly: that you are taking time to care for yourself. Sometimes you can't avoid someone completely, such as if they are a family member, nor do you have to. Simply find ways to reduce the time as you feel drawn to, from your own rising clarity and discernment.

This naturally opens up the space for you to lean in to spending more time with people who *do* help to light up your energy and your heart. Seek them out. Strengthen those connections.

Be aware, be discerning, tap into the intuitive guidance of your growing heart intelligence, and above all, take care of your own heart. As your incredible heart continues to awaken, you will be a light for others and in the world.

SINCERITY: IMPORTANT HEART QUALITY

One of the most important first steps to overcome heaviness and darkness is sincerity. You have to sincerely want to grow, to shift, to change. Sincerity aligns with surrender, which means that you come into this moment with humility and openness. Being humble and open is powerful, because you then clearly see for yourself that the old ways aren't really working. And that's when you create breakthroughs.

Sincerity gives you energy when you want to give up, when you want to stay in patterns even when you know they make you miserable. Sincerity helps you focus on living in new patterns that do take some effort to establish.

If you're sincere and channel that sincerity into focus, attention, and committed action to follow these heart-based tools, you will be rewarded with the awakening of the enormous power of your heart's intelligence. And all aspects of your life will vastly change for the better.

HEART EMBODIMENT:
Lifestyle Tips to Support and Transcend the Dark Heart

The following are some practical lifestyle tips and tools you can also incorporate to further support your brilliant heart's journey at this time and into further awakening beyond the Dark Heart phase:

- **Drink cacao and cinnamon elixirs.** Plants, even so-called common ones, have energetic influence and power. I love incorporating elixirs, or "potions" made of a specific mix of beneficial ingredients, into all my clients' regimens. They are an effective way to deliver nutrients right into your body. This warming elixir includes raw cacao, which contains bliss-promoting neurochemicals, as well as cinnamon, which is known to be a warming and digestion-enhancing spice, and can help to wake up your connection to your heart and get you out of your head. Use a base of nut milk, such as coconut or hemp, so it's creamy and adds some stabilizing fat. This elixir can be especially beneficial in the middle of your day, say midmorning or midafternoon. (See the Resources section or my website for many elixir and other recipes.)

- **Add omega fats.** These are healthy, grounding fats for the heart and the brain. Heart-healthy foods and brain-healthy foods are often the same! Omega fats are also associated with helping to boost moods and relieve depression. Incorporating seeds like chia, flax, and hemp, and nuts like walnuts and almonds, into your diet, as well as considering an algae-based DHA/EPA supplement, are great, clean sources.

- **Try light therapy.** Light, especially natural sunlight, is essential for health and well-being as well as feeling connected to the earth, nature, and the abundant Light that is essentially within us and all around us. If you feel down or disconnected, get more sunlight into your life (in safe amounts for your skin type). If that's not always possible, try a light that simulates the sun or some kind of light therapy box or device.

- **Spend more time outdoors.** Nature is expansive, like heart energy, and so being in nature is a way to feel expanded and get out of constricted, mind-based perspectives. Make space to read, sit, talk or walk with loved ones, or simply be in nature, whether that's a local park or a beach. If you live in an urban place, consider making your vacations or weekend getaways, when possible, in more natural spaces.

- **Ingest greens and concentrated greens daily.** Greens are truth, greens can powerfully help to support the opening of your heart, and greens are mineral- and antioxidant-rich as well as wonderful for your overall vitality! Colors impart a certain vibration, and green has traditionally been associated with the color of the *anahata* heart chakra, considered to be supportive of heart energy from a yogic standpoint.

- **Try incorporating greens like spinach, cilantro, kale, chard, and so on into your diet.** It's also an amazing energy and vitality booster to incorporate a concentrated greens powder every day, which includes "super" plants, rich in nourishing, protective qualities, and can even help to draw out heavy metals that weigh you down. Look for formulas that are properly balanced and that contain efficacious amounts of each ingredient versus containing negligible amounts of dozens of ingredients. (There are several great formulas out there. I am partial to the one I created, of course, which is created with careful intention, much passion for plants, and great love! You can check it out in the Resources section or on my site if you're interested.)

Key Points of the Dark Heart: Incoherence

- The Dark Heart stage is a stage of disconnection from the heart. This means that the heart and brain communication is cut off, so that the mind is mostly leading life.

- The Dark Heart incoherence results in confusion, frustration, stress, self-doubt, overwhelm, fear, anger, blame, unawareness, negative emotions, negative behaviors, or perhaps not feeling at all.

- This stage prompts us to move toward more self-awareness and growth through challenges.

- Heart coherence means creating more aligned, syncing up of communication between your heart, brain, and nervous system. This creates greater health, efficiency of your bodily systems, slower aging, higher immunity, mental clarity, and productivity.

- Heart coherence also leads to more calmness, clarity, peace, higher access to intuition, and more access to the heart emotions at will, which include appreciation, love, compassion, and joy.

- The more you grow your heart coherence, the more you will be able to shift negative thoughts to positive ones, not from forced positive thinking but with the power of accessing more heart emotions.

- Your heart produces an electromagnetic field that is 100 times stronger than the one your brain produces. You can sense the field and other people's "vibe," and they can sense your field and "vibe"!

- The more you practice the HeartAlign Meditation (see the Resources section to access the audio tracks) and the other practices offered in this book, the more you will increase your heart coherence and be able to transform your life.

As you continue your journey to awaken your heart intelligence, you will notice something: More and more energy is arising from inside of you. It was always available, but as incoherence continues to transform into coherence—in the way of greater energy, calmness, and clarity—you are about to increasingly feel and access that energy.

This means you are naturally shifting from the Dark Heart into the Propelled Heart. Let's learn about this next heart stage.

Our journey is just beginning!

Chapter 4

STAGE 2

THE PROPELLED HEART:
THE BEGINNING OF
COHERENCE

As you emerge from the darkness, you begin to experience a whole new reality known as the Propelled Heart. The transition to this stage feels exciting because you can actually start to feel more of your own incredible energic potential on a whole new level.

As you enter this stage from the Dark Heart, it can feel like you removed a bunch of heavy rocks from your pockets and cleaned fog from the lenses of your eyes. This may feel either quite sudden or that it built up slowly. Either way, it's fantastically liberating to get off the couch with all your newfound energy or move past a period of feeling down.

You may ask, "Where *did* all this energy come from?" In reality, this vitality was always within you. It emerged as heart-brain communication began to build and created a higher baseline of coherence in you, through realizations, new awareness, practicing the HeartAlign Meditation and other tools, and perhaps adopting healthier lifestyle habits that supported your awakening heart. This has now given you the power to access more of your own energy.

Sri Yukteswar says of the Propelled Heart stage, "His heart then becomes propelled to learn the real nature of the universe and, struggling to clear his doubts, seeks for evidence to determine what is truth."[28] The Propelled Heart is therefore by nature a state of great action. This action is driven by a deep inner struggle to figure out meaning in life, what is true, and what to do with our energy and with our lives in general.

THE JOURNEY OF SEEKING

As I shared with you earlier, I was on the road backpacking for three years. The first year and a half was pretty chaotic: I was chasing adventures like full moon parties in Thailand, deep water scuba diving in Malaysia, bicycling across villages in Southwest China, and exploring underground rivers in the Philippines. It was a constant feeling of seeking the next thing, as in *What's next? What's bigger and crazier and more exciting?* It was restlessness personified. And it was also starting to get a little reckless. At one point, I dove into the deep pool under a waterfall in Laos, trying to find a way to swim through an underground tunnel that I saw a local do. I got stuck and lost down in the underwater rocks, and thankfully just as I was starting to panic and run out of air, that same local dove in, grabbed my shoulders, and guided me through the tunnel.

I drove and camped across over nine countries before encountering an issue traveling to Mozambique. The roads were so bad that I had to come up with another plan. I ended up leaving my car (that I bought cheaply and sold after the adventure moved to another continent) at a hostel in

Johannesburg. I met a fellow traveler going up the coast to Inhambane, and she agreed to let me hitch a ride. The only thing was that I had to ride the entire way sitting in the open bed of her pickup truck. Thankfully she did have a mattress laid down back there, so though it was still tremendously bumpy at times, I saw it all as part of the fun.

Somewhere along that 13-hour drive, I put on my headphones and listened to the song "Learning to Fly" by Pink Floyd. Something clicked in, and I suddenly had the expansive feeling of being completely free. There I was, dusty and dirty on the back of that pickup truck, with only a little backpack to count as my worldly belongings, and absolutely no plan for my life. And yet I felt like I was flying! I felt incredibly full and yet incredibly light at the same time. The feeling was definitely centered in my heart, throbbing in and out of my chest and up to the back of my throat and crown of my head, and down into my belly, and in all directions out of my body. It was a kind of spiritual epiphany.

That moment shifted the trajectory of my journey, and my life. It was such a dramatically different feeling that I had never experienced until right then. Up until that point, most of my life felt confined. I could never escape feeling oppressed by trying to define myself by external achievements and what others thought of me in order to be good enough, and worthy of attention and validation and love. And I still hadn't been able to shake those feelings in those early, wild backpacking days, which as I look back, were more about trying to run away from those very feelings of uneasiness. That moment though, gave me a peek into what experiencing freedom in life actually felt like. *Real* freedom! A freedom I had read about in places like popular Rumi poems, but that I had never ever touched myself.

Never doubt that your life, your perspective of life, *everything,* can change in a moment. It did for me.

That experience opened the door to a lifelong journey that continues to this day—a journey that is an internal one and centered around inner growth, no matter where my body happens to be. After my African adventures, I was called to India, where I spent many months. I was open and fresh, with many layers peeled off around my identity that was tied to achievements and external validation. Well to be clear, it was largely peeled off at least for that time. The journey of shedding false ego identities continues to this day, as it does for pretty much all of us, as this is the core of the journey of being human, and also awakening the heart.

They say when the student is ready a teacher appears, and I was most certainly ready. It was in that period that I went to the spiritual city of Rishikesh, wandered into a bookshop, and came across a small blue book called *The Universality of Yoga* by Paramahansa Yogananda, the yogi mentioned here and throughout *You Are More Than You Think You Are.*

Yogananda's books introduced me to the concepts of the True Self, Kriya yoga, and oneness; and his teachings bridged and unified concepts around universal truth and love that deeply resonated with me. It hit me like a ton of bricks, and from that point on, the journey went many layers deeper. Though I stopped wandering so much around the world, it was in that worldwide journey that I did find what I was looking for—or at least the *place* to find what I was looking for. It was right inside me, in my heart the whole time!

This inner struggle and seeking I experienced is part of the universal experience of the Propelled Heart. There is a whole lot of thinking and analyzing at this heart stage, such as: *Which diet and lifestyle am I supposed to follow? Should I be doing more? How do I become more successful right away? What is the best way for me to lose the weight? Am I in the right career— or should I change again? I still don't look good enough—how do I look better?* The Propelled Heart is the stage where motivational speakers, dietary programs, new gadgets and devices, biohacking, life hacks, self-help books, and other ways to improve yourself become especially interesting.

Seeking is by nature restless energy. It's great to be productive of course, but restless energy is different. Think of that wild horse mind, knocking over buckets of water and oats, as it runs itself ragged by running around in circles! Restless energy is like that—it's the gnawing feeling that we always *have* to be doing something, whether that is constant working, socializing, cleaning, tinkering, chatting, online surfing, or communicating in quiet moments. Can you relate to this? Or can you think of someone you would describe as restless? Restless energy makes feeling truly peaceful impossible. And when we're restless, guess what it often leads to? Anxiety and stress.

At its core, the energy of always seeking and doing and chasing means that we feel a deep sense of lack within ourselves. It means that we're still identifying with the feeling of needing to be fixed, to be "better" or do more in order to be good enough.

Society's messages often drive us to chase after more— money, fame, fashion, looks, followers, fans—because it tells us that's what we need to create success and happiness. But we come to experience for ourselves that it's all a fallacy of the ego and society, which largely reflects the ego mind. The truth is that these things can never give us the peace and joy that can only come from connecting to your heart and to who you really are. This inner connection will give you all that you are seeking. No achievement, material thing, "perfect" body shape, or award will ever be able to! It's okay to want to improve ourselves, and it's perfectly fine to want and to enjoy material things. But we should never give away our own power by allowing these external things to define our worth or who we are.

And the more you feel whole, which is the truth of your nature, the more abundant the energy is that runs through you and radiates out. And the more abundance you will see show up in your life, including more opportunities, helpful people, finances, expanded energy, meaningful relation-ships, and love. *That's because wholeness is abundance.* If you don't feel whole, you feel lack, and then more lack will show up in your life.

A surety, a confidence in yourself that is sturdy and increasingly impenetrable, rises up from feeling the whole-ness inside of yourself, which you can access through your heart. You realize that you no longer have to give away your power to anyone telling you your worth. Real confidence comes from the inside, and it doesn't go away no matter how our bodies age or change, if our popularity wanes, if our roles change in life (like our kids growing up and not needing our care in the same way), or if we get laid off from a job.

Your heart will teach you that you don't have to keep chasing. As you shift on the inside, more will come to *you.* And instead of being known as someone who has obtained or achieved certain things, you become known for simply being a wonderful person that others have to meet and want to be around.

STAGE 2   The Propelled Heart: The Beginning of Coherence

Practice: Experiencing Your Abundant Wholeness

Your heart can teach you how to actually feel whole, how to be in touch with the immensely powerful energy within you that cannot be seen with the physical eyes.

This practice is designed to help you experience this very power in this moment. As you start to come into contact with it, even for brief moments, you increasingly come to realize that the lack was never real. It felt real when you were up in your head, but your heart's brilliant intelligence is pointing out the truth: *You are whole as you are.* And deepening into that knowing is where you will start to experience authentic confidence—and incredible leaps of abundance across your whole life.

To do this practice:

- Find a comfortable seat.

- Shift your awareness to your heart. You can place both hands over your physical heart if it helps you to focus your full awareness there.

- Imagine your heart as the sun, radiating out a brilliant light in all directions. Imagine your heart as the sun within you, shining out its natural, incredible light. The sun knows no lack. The sun simply is exactly as it is, in its brilliant glory, whole and radiant. This is the same truth within you, which you can tangibly experience through connecting to the nature of your amazing heart. It doesn't need anyone to approve, because it's so full within itself.

- Bask in your heart's brilliant light, the energy of radiant wholeness that is the core of your True Self, for at least a few minutes. This is teaching you, through direct experience, the truth of your nature. You can't think or analyze your way to feeling whole and abundant and

without lack; you actually have to let your
heart intelligence teach you. It's a profound
wisdom that is beyond words and beyond the
linear ego mind. You have to experience it.

Enjoy this practice daily at any time. The more you
practice it, the more deeply you can begin to embody
your abundant True Self. At first, it might be hard to connect to that light or feeling of wholeness within you, and
that's okay too. Deeply connecting to your heart, as you
would in any relationship, may take some time and also
consistent attention, even for a few moments in your
morning and through your day. It will come. It is in there!

This practice can be especially beneficial as an
add-on to your HeartAlign Meditation, after you've
gone through those prior steps, to further help you tune
in to your heart's power, or to practice it in your quiet
moments, or anytime you feel a sense of self-doubt or
lack creeping in. Remember: There is a fullness, a wholeness in your heart that is the core of you. You actually
need nothing else or to get anywhere in order to be
good enough. You already have it; you only have to realize it. And then abundance across your life will follow.

DISCOVERING YOUR WISDOM
BEYOND OVERTHINKING

The Propelled Heart is still in the mind a lot, and the
heart's wisdom can easily be drowned out. We want to
avoid confusion and depleting ourselves by going in one
direction and then the next, and endlessly wondering
and questioning ourselves as to whether we are doing the
right thing or making the right decision. Think of the wild
horse mind this time as running in circles clockwise, and
then exactly in the same circle but counterclockwise. It's so
exhausting and doesn't get us where we want to be.

Choosing to follow my heart over my head led me to the greatest love of my life, my husband, Jon. Our first dinner date was at a scenic beachside restaurant, just three days after we first met. We ordered salads and veggie pizza, but Jon expanded his order to include a large meatball platter for "Meatball Monday," complemented by prosciutto with melon and an extra serving of burrata cheese. He revealed with a wide smile, "I always order three dishes for myself." I paled a bit and smiled thinly. For years I had followed a plant-based diet, and for the most part I had dated people who had similar eating habits—and portion sizes! A little voice of doubt sounded off in my head: *Ugh! Maybe we aren't really compatible.*

Some of Jon's tattoos also gave me pause. It didn't bother me that they covered almost his entire body except for his neck and head. But some of them seemed a bit interesting, perhaps immature by my mind's judgment. My heart, though, encouraged me to look deeper, to dive beneath the surface. I realized that, like Jon, I had gone through numerous phases of growth myself; mine just weren't imprinted on my skin. More importantly, as we talked and laughed through the night, I recognized that our core values—honesty, reliability, and loyalty—were in perfect alignment. "All right fine," I said to myself, "I see him. And he sees me. We connect on the big stuff, and isn't that what really matters?"

As the night concluded, Jon told me he loved me, for the first time! And I realized that the connection I felt with Jon was undeniable. My heart and gut's intuition drew me irresistibly toward him, overpowering any doubts my mind tried to present. There was no way I was going to let apprehension and fear get in the way of this love!

True wellness means to be in a state where we are in deep connection with ourselves, and we make choices that align with us in any given moment. This means taking information and discerning what feels right and simply trusting that. How do we discern, exactly? You don't listen to the wild horse mind but instead filter the information through your heart and your body, which you will learn in practice. Intuitive knowing will start to arise as guidance from deep within you, which will become easier for you to hear over time.

I had a client who wouldn't eat anything unless she texted me first, whether she was at a restaurant or at home, and I approved her food choices. She also texted me when something triggered her into not feeling safe—like when people left rude comments on her social media. She struggled to feel secure in herself, and this fear played out with her feeling safer when others made her choices instead. She relied on her agents and manager to call the shots in her career with little of her own input, and she relied on her nannies to guide the parenting style of her kids.

Our work was centered on establishing trust—self-trust that is. It started by her cooking some simple things for herself, guiding her to tune in to her own intuition about what was most nourishing for her to choose and eat in that moment. We also focused on incorporating deep belly breathing, meditation, learning to tune in to her own intuition, deep down in her heart and in her gut. Over time, the texting became less, and her self-reliance and connection to inner safety grew. Today, she has far more self-trust, is far more in tune with her own intuition, and makes (mostly) her own decisions about what to eat, how to parent, and what to do in her career. This is the true confidence behind her beautiful smile now.

What's true for you may not be true for others. And what's true for them might not be true for you, and it's all okay! Part of transcending the trappings of the Propelled Heart and coming into peace means that we bypass seeing our way of doing things as the "right way." This creates the heart block of pride. And pride depletes much of our energy in trying to defend, convince, and get the validation from others. We need to convince no one of our own truth. It's enough for us to know our truth, and there is great power and peace in needing that alone.

The following practice will help to put you in touch with living your truth in daily decisions small and large, which is a key part of holistic wellness and achieving true health.

Practice: Heart-Gut Alignment to Get in Touch with Your Body

When you're truly present, you can access true wisdom. It may have felt impossible until this point to really feel that, with all the wild horse mind thinking! So we must keep dropping deeper, down into your heart and your body. We bypass the thoughts. Your heart and your body are portals to take you into pure, true presence.

The present moment is where you can create your highest health. It's where you tap into your highest potential and make the best decisions. It's where you can overcome mindless eating, stress eating, and overeating. It's where you transcend fear and access deep, intuitive knowing, which leads to peace and immense creativity.

We must be present to have more clarity and make better daily decisions. This includes in your family and work life as well as how best to take care of your body and yourself. When I work one-on-one with clients, most of them tell me that they honestly have no idea when they are truly hungry or what their body is telling them it needs. And they often experience a lot of anxiety and self-doubt about making decisions, such as what to say yes or no to.

For example, I taught this practice to a type A, high-performance client, whom I will call Madelyn, who was living a pretty robotic existence when we met. She stuck to a strict schedule with no nuance. She ate pretty much the same few meal choices, did the same gym routine, and went about her work in the same exact ways every day . . . for years! She told me she did this because she was anxious that if she strayed from her schedule in any way, she might do things "wrong."

By practicing this Heart-Gut Alignment Practice, she began to shift her foods more seasonally and on certain days, eating more densely in the winter, for example, and more salads in the summer. She varied up her exercise—sometimes trying a new Pilates class or going on a walk with friends, or letting herself rest during times she felt she needed it. Madelyn was thrilled to experience more natural energy, brighter skin, less aches and pains, and better sleep, and she even reduced some medications. This more flexible, softened version of herself allowed her to pursue new and different ways to develop strategies and communicate with people on her team, which created even greater success.

Instead of getting stuck in your head, you're traveling deep into the core of your body and yourself. In your body lies the ability to sense pure awareness in this moment, with clarity and deep wisdom of what is needed now. This practice is going to wake up your heart intelligence to create somatic or body awareness. You do that by shifting your awareness into your heart and then taking that deeper, expanded awareness down into your body, especially your gut.

There are neurons and neurotransmitters in the gut as well, making it also a kind of brain. The vagus nerve is the longest cranial nerve in the body, running from your brain down to your large intestine. It is part of your parasympathetic nervous system and sends information between your heart, brain, and digestive system. Your gut can help communicate with the lower brain centers, activating some of the more primal instincts, as in our gut reactions.[29] The gut also houses the solar plexus, or *manipura* chakra, which Vedic and yogic philosophy teaches to be the seat of our personal power.

When you do this practice and breathe with your heart and gut as one unit, while self-generating the positive heart emotion of appreciation, *you align the brain in your gut with the brain in your heart*. The heart will then automatically harmonize the communication between your head and your heart[30] and will help you effectively listen to your body's deep wisdom for itself.

Try doing this practice, which will take under one minute, before you make a decision about which direction to go in, which next best step to take, what to eat, or before you make any self-care or other decision, to access your own deep intelligence and wisdom to guide you to the best choice.

Here are the steps:

- **Place one hand on your heart and one hand on your belly or your gut, just over your belly button.** Take a few deep, slow breaths. Place your full awareness on these areas of your body. Feel your beating heart and the breath traveling all the way down into your belly.

- **Next, take a few deep breaths, imagining that you are breathing in and out of the entire area as one unit, from your heart all the way down to your belly.** Connect these powerful centers of your body—your heart and belly— through your breath as one energetic unit.

- **Continue to breathe deeply in this way as you self-generate a feeling of appreciation.** You self-generate appreciation by recalling someone or something that makes you tap into the feeling, which is a mix of gratitude, awe, and approval. It can be a loved one or a special past event. Focus on the expansive feeling of appreciation and release the person or event once you tap in, to help you move past limited mind patterns into openness.

- **Now ask your heart-gut unit a question.** Go ahead and ask this deep, core part of you the question to the answer you are seeking. It can be, *What is the right decision to make here? Should I say yes or no? What should I eat right now? What is it that I need? How should I best care for myself right now?* It may sound funny asking a question to yourself, but it's to prompt you to unlock the answer from a deeper place inside of you.

- **Act on the insight you receive from your heart-gut.** From deep within your center, listen to any guidance that surfaces. Do not try to obtain this answer from a mental place. Focus on your heart-gut for the answer. Over time and with practice, you will be able to more easily hear these answers from your body as intuitive knowing, or deeper insights. You might intuit a personal or business decision or direction to take. Or that your body needs a hot meal instead of a salad, or a salad instead of a heavier meal. Your body might tell you that it needs to rest, or that it needs to move. It might tell you that even though your best friend is doing some new program and wants you to come along, it isn't right for you.

While you can gather facts, ultimately you are the one who holds the wisdom for deciding what is best for you. And you can access this wisdom whenever you want, by moving past the overthinking mind and tapping into your heart intelligence and into your own body's guidance.

LETTING GO OF TRYING TO CONTROL LIFE

Since the Propelled Heart at its core is struggling to find meaning and truth, as Sri Yukteswar taught, it often makes plans. Plans can feel comforting. Plans, such as what we are doing the next few weekends, the five-year trajectory, the age when we will get married or buy a house, and a detailed career path can make us feel like we have a concrete direction. The mind likes that, because direction and plans create a sense of safety and security, while unknowns feel scary to the linear mind. The mind also likes when others agree with our plans and ideas, because it reinforces a feeling of security that our path is "right."

Plans can be helpful, of course, and there's practical benefit to getting schedules and basic timelines organized. But issues arise when we create strong expectations that our plans and life *must* go exactly as we expect. We can create a rigid sense of seriousness and importance around these plans.

Trying to control and overly plan your life is ultimately lack-thinking and cuts off your abundance. Control narrows things down to a specific way, which might feel safe to the ego, but it's really not. Instead, when we are open, we are connected to the whole, which means amazing things and opportunities can show up in infinite ways that the little mind can't possibly plan for! When we stop trying to force our way, we open up instead. Openness is a *huge* part of abundance.

It was when I was walking around in the world, feeling abundant, clear, and open, that I bumped into Deepak Chopra on the street, literally, on the corner of 16th Street and Union Square East, in New York City. I seized the opportunity! I went right up to him and reminded him that even though we had not met in person, he had just generously reviewed my third book, *The Beauty Detox Power.*

This one encounter led to us connecting more in the coming weeks and months, which then led to us co-authoring a book called *Radical Beauty*. I could not even have conceived of these amazing occurrences from my thinking, analyzing mind!

So it's key to dissolve control tendencies in order to blast past perceived limitations and open up energy and abundance in your life. And it's also key in order to reduce stress in your life, which is an enormous way to also open up more vitality and energy all around!

Let's start to dismantle control tendencies with some awareness. First of all, as we all know, life does not always cooperate with our big plans anyway. *Uh oh.* When life doesn't stick to the plan, you feel a trigger, a sensation, a feeling of being thrown off in some way. If you pay attention, you will notice that triggers provoke physical changes in your body. Your heart rate may speed up, or the tone of your voice may become sharper or faster. Perhaps your body tightens or starts moving in a more hurried or stiff way.

While triggers are felt as sensations in the body, resistance is created in the mind. The mind says, *Wait, this isn't part of the plan! I don't like this.* Resistance takes many forms, including feeling upset, angry, irritated, frustrated, or excessively disappointed when our expectations for life aren't met.

In daily life, resistance looks like getting angry when the weather doesn't cooperate or there is traffic, becoming totally derailed when someone is late or completely disagrees with your way (say of raising your kids or a political opinion), or experiencing intense irritation when you expected the car keys to be in the kitchen basket and they are lost instead. In larger ways, it can mean feeling constant frustration from what can feel like the squeeze of pressure in life, such as when your expectation to meet someone and get married and have two kids by a certain age does not happen. Or when your career path doesn't play out exactly as you expected.

Resistance creates emotional turmoil and builds up tension in the body, which leads to stress responses in our bodies that over time disable us, age us, and break us down. It creates the internal disorder felt as stress and prevents the higher centers of your brain from working as efficiently as they should.[31] As we start to feel chaotic in our thoughts, our bodies then also move into chaos. Tension can be held in your diaphragm, which restricts deep breathing. You start taking more shallow breaths and feel more trapped in your thoughts. *Life* then starts to feel constricting and more challenging.

Sure, there are real challenges we have to deal with in life. Maybe we can't pay the upcoming rent that's due. There's a reality in front of us: We need to figure out the rent. We can enter into the resistance and stress response, as we just described, and break down our organs, lower our immunity, and be up all night worrying. For anyone whose ever tried these things (myself included), we can all attest that they do not help one little bit.

So what do we do instead? We harmonize with life. We accept that we can't control life and that's okay. It's okay because we can always use our heart intelligence and move forward with life in the best possible way, without all the unnecessary—and unhelpful—stress.

The more you harmonize with life, the better things will start to work out, and the more abundant your life is going to become. You're going to be amazed that there is a whole new way to go about things, the way of your powerful heart, and it's going to change everything!

HARMONY: TRUE STRESS RESILIENCE

If trying to control life creates stress, what creates the opposite, which is expansion and flow? Harmony.

Harmony is birthed from coherence. Coherence begins inside of us, with our heart syncing up with our brain, nervous system, and the rest of our bodily systems and organs. Harmony is then created, which extends that feeling of us syncing with events, people, and *all of life* as it shows up in each moment.

Harmony is an extension of wholeness—it's being in alignment and oneness with the whole, therefore making it a powerful state of abundance. Harmony is also true resilience, meaning you stay in your heart no matter what comes your way in your life, and you avoid moving into resistance or a stress response. You remain flexible and simply pivot and flow with life as it arises in each present moment. It's your heart saying, *This way is closed? No problem! Let's just go this other way!* And, *This didn't work out as planned—no worries, let's just adjust.* Harmonizing with life will create so much more lightness, abundance, and freedom in your life.

You simply choose what your heart guides you to be the best thing in that moment and go with it. Period. Harmony is created in each present moment instead of battling negative thoughts and upset born of resistance about how life is not meeting your plans and rigid expectations. The more you go the harmonious way, the more harmony becomes your default.

At the end of the day, who cares if the exact plans aren't met? Ego does. But if you engage your heart's intelligence and wise perspective, you will find that your heart doesn't care if the plans don't exactly work out. The heart can always show you the way to stay in harmony, calmness, and flow, even if it's a different path. And that's what really counts.

With harmony peace expands, and success does too. Goals always work out far better with harmony. Marriages work in a harmonious setting, and harmony breeds deep friendship. Businesses grow when there is harmony within its teams and harmonious communication with its customers. Harmony feels like everyone's needs get met in a calm, peaceful way. Instead of the right and the wrong way, it transforms into, "There's a way to make this win-win because we are all equal here." We drop the need to judge, defend, or try to convince others.

HARMONY STARTS WITHIN

No matter what the outer circumstances, no matter how you've believed that stress is inevitable, you can learn to create harmony and resilience in your life, from your heart outward. The more you live in peace within, the more you can find it in your environment. On the other hand, if you feel chaotic inside, you will see chaos in the world.

Harmony in your life originates in the heart. Your heart is the primary biological oscillator that sets the body's rhythms, a concept introduced in The Dark Heart chapter (Chapter 3). When you create coherence in your heart rhythm, you then start to generate entrainment, or harmony, across your nervous system and the other systems in your body.[32] Your nervous system is a big part of how you sense and feel safe in the world. Getting your nervous system under control has a major role in maintaining coherence and creating peace and harmony in your life. Yogananda even said, "If you have a calm nervous system, you will have success in everything you undertake."[33]

Harmony will change your body and your life. It will help you avoid experiencing and expressing anger, frustration, and irritation out into the world. It will enable you to communicate more effectively, build bridges and stronger connections with others, as well as more success-fully create whatever you want. Harmony will help dissolve stress eating, numbing with alcohol or screens, and other forms of hurting your body.

To understand how powerfully this works, let's first see how harmony, born of heart intelligence, can help you manage stress and see it from the evidence-based impact it has on your hormones. Hormones are your body's vital chemical messengers and affect many different processes in your body, including what your moods are like, and how you metabolize food, create babies, and sleep.

The stress response activates a whole cascade of hormones in your body, including cortisol, which is known as the stress hormone. Stress can induce chronically elevated levels of cortisol, which damages us in so many horrible ways. These include destroying brain cells,[34] inhib-iting skin growth and regeneration (this is why stress really does create wrinkles!),[35] increasing bone loss,[36] reducing glucose utilization,[37] and increasing fat accumulation (especially around the belly, waist, and hips).[38]

On the other hand, the hormone DHEA can reduce cortisol and help prevent depression, anxiety, and cardio-vascular disease; it has also been shown to help increase energy and vitality. DHEA also plays a role in optimal fer-tility. Research shows that by applying your own heart intelligence, you can positively shift your hormonal bal-ance by changing your perceptions and emotions.

The HeartMath Institute decided to test the heart's effect on hormones by running a study featuring a tech-nique designed to create heart coherence when you start to feel distress. In just one month of practicing the heart coherence tool, which also included shifting to the heart and self-generating positive heart emotions like appreciation, subjects increased an average of 100 percent in their DHEA levels and dropped an average of 23 percent in their cortisol levels.[39] This research is exciting because it shows that we can learn to empower ourselves to create hormonal balance within—without external aids, such as drugs!

The HeartAlign Harmonize Method and the tools presented in this book have incorporated some of this important research to increase heart coherence, along with ancient and intuitive wisdom to allow us to stay in the powerful place of harmony, and remain increasingly resilient against stress in daily life.

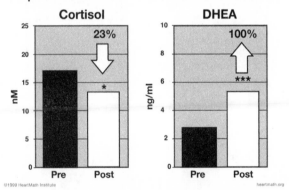

Improvements in hormone levels, indicated from a 100% rise of DHEA levels and a decrease in cortisol by 23%, after one month of practicing heart coherence tools. (Courtesy of the HeartMath Institute.)

The HeartAlign Harmonize Method

The HeartAlign Harmonize Method is a quick and efficient way to create harmony in each moment of daily life using your heart intelligence. It's adapted from HeartMath's techniques and research where, after becoming heart coherent, you directly connect to your heart's intuitive guidance to access your own internal wisdom. This creates a clear perspective of the most harmonious action step forward in any given situation, bypassing stress and confusing overthinking, and instead generating more abundant and successful outcomes.

This isn't a meditation. It's an on-the-spot technique that you can practice right in the midst of your life, which is where we have the potential to create harmony. It can be practiced in as little as *one minute* to help you access the power of your heart and shift from a negative or divisive mindset to a harmonious, coherent one.

Yogananda says, "He must first feel at home with himself, then he will find harmony in his interaction with all with whom he comes in contact."[40] If you've struggled to find harmony with others, especially those who trigger you or have different beliefs, this method will help you enormously.

You can practice this at your desk, in a restaurant, talking on the phone, or watching a baseball game. While some steps are similar to the HeartAlign Meditation, this approach is designed to help you adapt in real time, in the middle of your day, to make powerful shifts into more harmony in your everyday life. And the more you use it, the more harmonious and successful your life will become.

Here are the main steps:

1. Become aware of a trigger that creates resistance, a stress response, or any kind of disharmonious reaction.

2. Relax your body.

3. Shift your awareness into your heart and take a few slow, deep breaths; imagine you are breathing in and out of your heart.

4. Self-generate the feeling of appreciation, by recalling a person or an event that helps you tap into this expansive feeling.

5. Seek heart intelligence on how to create harmony in the moment or situation.

6. Act on your heart's guidance.

An expanded explanation of each step follows:

1. **Become aware of a trigger that creates resistance, a stress response, or any kind of disharmonious reaction.** Recognize the physical sensations and cues when you are pulled out of harmony, out of feeling calm. Notice your heart rhythm speeding up or your breaths starting to feel more shallow. Maybe you notice your shoulders or stomach tense or tighten. Be alert.

    If you have already entered a form of resistance, such as feeling upset or speaking sharply to someone, closing your heart, or judging others, try to pause as soon as you can. Then proceed with the rest of these steps.

2. **Relax your body.** Relax your body by practicing Yogananda's method of tensing and relaxing all the muscles of the body three times that we incorporated in the HeartAlign Meditation in the Dark Heart: Incoherence chapter (Chapter 3). Or you can simply take a big breath in, and with a big exhale, relax your whole body and imagine releasing all tightness and pent-up tension. The more relaxed your body is, the easier it is to maintain or restore harmony and coherence.

3. **Shift your awareness into your heart and take a few slow, deep breaths; imagine you are breathing in and out of your heart.** Shift your awareness to your heart. Forget the trigger and everything else in life as you tune in to your true power center: your heart. Remember that shifting

your focus to your heart enhances heart-brain communication, restores nervous system balance, and promotes emotional coherence.[41] Keep your anchor in your heart by taking deep, slow breaths, imagining that you are breathing in and out of your heart. Deep, slow breathing helps you maintain coherence and connectedness to your inner power when triggers, disharmony, and stress responses begin to arise.

4. **Self-generate the feeling of appreciation.** Generate a sense of appreciation in this very moment. This means recalling some go-to past events or loved ones that help you tap into the expansive feeling of appreciation in the middle of life. Even if you sustain the feeling of appreciation for only 10 seconds or so, it plays a crucial role in neutralizing negative reactions.

5. **Seek heart intelligence on how to create harmony in the moment or the situation.** Maintain your focus on your heart and request inner guidance. You can directly ask your heart, "What should I do or say to create harmony in this situation?" or "What should I do here to create the best, most harmonious outcome?" Feel what your heart has to tell you in the way of intuitive insights and calm, practical solutions that arise. Remember that your heart contains a high-powered intelligence that will give you the answers when you sincerely seek and tune in. Like any method, the more you practice asking your heart and listening for an answer, the more clearly you will be able to recognize the messages from your heart intelligence.

The messages from your heart may give you a feeling, such as guidance, on what to do or validate something you already knew. Often you will find a shift in perception, and sometimes your heart will tell you something your ego might not like, such as "Just let it go." Stay open to what comes up.

6.   **Act on your heart's guidance.** The right action is going to arise from your heart. But you have to retrain yourself and bring in patience to learn to hear—and act on—your heart's intelligence.

It's really important to *take action* on your heart's guidance to steer your decisions, actions, and words. Focus on slowing down instead of pushing forward in an automated way. It takes strength not to just react in the same way, but if you keep going through the steps with sincerity, you will break free from limiting patterns and make incredible shifts in your life.

Still, even as you start to hear your heart, you might not listen. Sometimes you choose to go the other way, because certain patterns of thinking, seeing things, and reacting may feel greatly challenging to change. And that's okay. You are building your awareness of what is and what isn't heart intelligence. And that awareness is key to shifting your behaviors and your life, even if it takes some time. It's a journey.

This practice taught me that a key part of creating more harmony, day to day in my life, was more letting go. My heart showed me that I could let go more of misunderstandings, careless comments I used to take so personally, like the elderly person we see in our community who sometimes laughs and makes comments about my sons' long hair. I used to feel red-hot anger and want to say something rude to her. Now I see she's just the way she is, and I tell my boys she's just used to different hair where she is from, and it's no big deal for people to have their little opinions. My heart showed me that I could let go of micromanaging the building of our new website, how much screen time my husband was letting our kids have when I was away at a meeting, and a million other things. This led to an increased flow of energy, and peace across my day that was incredible.

I taught a simplified version to my older son, who used to dread—and constantly complain about—the challenging Friday nature hikes his class takes. Instead of resisting, I taught him to relax, go into his heart and tap into the feeling of appreciation, and then go into the hikes with a more neutral mindset. Guess what? The complaining largely disappeared! He said the hikes were not so difficult after all, and he was even excited to get a new pair of hiking boots for them!

The more you practice this method, the more empowered you'll be to shift your reactions and create more harmony as your baseline, go-to way of being in the world. This will ultimately, transform your life in a major way.

**Important Times to Do the
HeartAlign Harmonize Method**

- As you flow through your day, making
  small and larger decisions alike
  and interacting with others

- Anytime you have a choice or decision
  to make that you aren't sure of

- In addressing home and family decisions and
  dealings, when assessing what is best for all

- In handling work decisions and dealings,
  when multiple people and personalities are
  involved, and assessing what is best for all

- In handling situations with
  people who challenge you

- Before responding to a comment, e-mail,
  text, or so on that triggers you

- Transitioning from your workday to
  downtime or time with your loved
  ones, to leave work energy behind

- At the end of the day as part of your
  evening routine, to review the day and find
  some internal resolution to situations you
  may still have to further address, so that
  you can rest and sleep more deeply

IS THE HEART REALLY SPEAKING?
OR IS IT THE EGO?

One of the most important and practical skills you can develop across your life is being able to determine whether your heart is giving you the messages or if they are coming from the ego. This is crucial because it will cut out the overthinking and the rigid, negative thoughts and expectations that lead to stress and block the flow of abundance coming to you. This skill will make the HeartAlign Harmonize Method increasingly effective for you.

Being in touch with the energetic heart, an access point for the True Self, is pure medicine for the Propelled Heart. As the energetic heart continues to open, intuitive deeper knowing replaces the overthinking and confusion. Your life will change. It will become simpler and far more peaceful.

The ego can often be mistaken for the heart. But remember that strong, erratic emotions and thoughts that feel narrow, divisive, or judgmental are the ego. This is definitely not the heart's intelligence. Ego's way feels rigid and often sees someone as wrong or the loser. Some examples of this are seeing someone else's diet, parenting approach, and political or religious affiliations as wrong, and yours is right. This can block your connecting to some amazing people who could really elevate your life.

The heart is enormously calm and has an expansive energy. It feels like you are zooming out from an event to see a broader perspective, one that shows you the way to win-win solutions. Sometimes the heart's messages are quite subtle. It's like placing a seashell to your ear and listening, intently, for the sounds in there. It's a tuning in. It's not going to scream at you, so you do need to consciously listen.

Listening to your heart can feel like wordless realizations or inner guidance. Your heart may speak to you a little differently, perhaps in the form of words or images rising up in your consciousness. In any case, stay open and alert, and you will begin to hear—and listen—better and better. Listening to your heart's intelligence, which is always available to you, is a life-changing skill to develop!

Does a thought or a decision bring you peace? If so, it will be from the heart. Not every decision is going to feel good, but there will be a sense of peace. Sometimes there is a sense of pain, grief, or loss along with the peace, but underlying peace will be there, always.

There usually won't be a lot of narrative or story, just what is. If your thought or actions don't bring you peace, and there's a lot of talk that goes along with it, like defending your decision or position, or judging, ego is still at play. And it's not a decision that comes from the heart. When it's not of the heart, disharmony is created; there will be more to clean up later and energy will be wasted.

It becomes easier and part of your life to live from your heart the more you do this. It will help you slow down and see another way to harmony. Your mind and thoughts never did that. You're going to love heart-based living as you incorporate it into your life. Your life will work better, more and more. Ultimately, your heart's power will guide you away from the perils of instant gratification and toward the long-term happiness, peace, and fulfillment that are created from growing coherence.

When your friend snaps at you for no reason, your ego tells you to ignore her for days. But your heart tells you to put aside your own hurt and approach her with compassion. You learn she was worried about some medical test results she just received. You easily forgive the snappiness, which had nothing to do with you, and instead you turn your attention to how you can support her. The expanded perspective of heart intelligence allows you to care and be there for your friend. You also avoid drama, unnecessary stressful emotions, and heart-brain incoherence. Instead, nourishing connection and coherence grow in your life, and to those around you, including your friend.

You start to see two choices: following the old, automated pattern that you've been stuck in, or the path of peace and lightness that is the way of your heart. Over time, following your heart's intelligence becomes easier the more you purposely shift into your heart, and you then start to see that your life simply works better. You get along better with others, and you enjoy more success at work and in all your relationships.

Gandhi Teaches Us the Difference between the Heart and the Head

Gandhi's greatest power in leading India to independence from the British was his inner voice: "A little voice within us tells us, You are on the right track, move neither to your left nor right, but keep to the straight and narrow way. It has never failed me, and for that matter anyone else. And everyone who wills can hear the voice. It is within everyone."[42]

American journalist Vincent Sheean once asked Gandhi how he felt so certain of listening to his inner voice. Sheean said, "Others have inner voices and are not sure."[43] He seemed to be alluding to whether the voice within was really from the heart, or the True Self, of Spirit from within, or from the ego or the limited mind.

Gandhi replied that "the [renunciation] precedes the certainty."[44] Gandhi was essentially saying that only *once he had surrendered his own desires* could he be certain that the guidance of the inner voice was coming from his heart, or Spirit speaking to him through the heart, versus a projection of his ego. In learning and adhering to this important heart intelligence skill, Gandhi was able to lean on the reliable guidance of his heart time and time again.

"Great leaders are great followers. They strive to surrender their own attachments and hungers so they can gain guidance from the universe through their inner voice," writes Hitendra Wadhwa, professor at Columbia Business School in his book *Inner Mastery, Outer Impact*.[45] This was true of Gandhi.

How do we surrender? When we seek guidance from our heart, through the HeartAlign Harmonize Method and other tools, we surrender to its all-powerful wisdom. We surrender more and more to the little messages or guidance that comes from our own inner voice, rising up from our heart. Just become more aware. You will increasingly become more in tune with your heart's amazing intelligence.

TRANSFORMING YOUR
RELATIONSHIP WITH TIME

The Propelled Heart can feel much stress from time pressure. The mind tells you to rush to fit more in, do more, to get from place to place. You may feel the squeeze of not having enough hours in the day to get it all in, or so you tell yourself. Chaotic thoughts that are not synced with the heart create "hurry energy." Hurry energy makes you feel you have to speed up. This in turn creates faster, disordered heart rhythm patterns and further throws off your heart-brain communication and nervous system balance. Suddenly, we are fed a flurry of thoughts pushing us to move even faster, telling us we are not doing enough. That *we* are not enough.

The heart has its own calm rhythm, which is highly intelligent and therefore highly efficient. It never needs to get swept into the rhythm of the busy world around. The truth is that you will get pretty much the same things done in the same time, either with the frantic stressful energy of rushing that wreaks havoc on your body and peace, or without it. I know that if I get caught up in a mad pace during the morning lunch-making, breakfast-making, driving to school routine, things feel *so* much more hard— and I feel far more exhausted by 8:00 A.M. versus when I stay calm!

Learn to live from the calm rhythm of your heart. This is actually the most truly efficient rhythm, for in its profound intelligence, it can find the best solutions in an intuitive, nonlinear way when you don't block its power.

When you start to feel rushed, focusing on getting more heart coherent is the most important thing! Shift to your heart, and take a few deep, slow breaths, as you've learned to do with the HeartAlign practices so far. Take even a few seconds to expand out of the present situation, which may feel like it's constricting you, by focusing on the energy of appreciation.

Making this little heart shift in the middle of being aware that you are experiencing "hurry energy" helps you reemerge back into that moment of life, feeling calmer and more centered. Remind yourself that you don't have to rush or hurry. You just have to do things with care and present-moment attention, and then things will work out in the best possible way.

HEART EMBODIMENT:
Lifestyle Tips to Support and
Transcend the Propelled Heart

The following are some practical lifestyle tips and tools I recommend to further support your heart's journey right now and into further awakening beyond the Propelled Heart phase:

- Nurture your gut health daily. It's absolutely critical to take care of all your "brains"—the one in your head, the one in your heart, and the one in your gut! Gut health is vital to overall wellness, sustaining more positive moods, and mental and physical health, including better digestion and immunity. Your physical health is one of the keys to unlocking your heart. You need vitality and energy to go through the process, and you want to avoid distracting aches, pains, and various energy-draining disorders as much as possible. It's important to eat lots of fiber, which helps to modulate your gut and create the short-chain fatty acids that reduce overall inflammation. It's important that you are eliminating regularly, an important way to build and sustain youthful energy and health. We can't be full of vitality if we are full of garbage and junk!

A way to take care of your gut is by taking probiotics every day, as healthy bacteria can get wiped out by stress, sugar, less-than-ideal foods, and many facets of modern living. I have long been a passionate advocate of aligning to nature in the way of gut health and other aspects of lifestyle protocols, as we are all part of nature. As such, I am partial to soil-based organism (SBO) probiotics, which emulate how our ancestors used to consume a little bit of soil on unwashed fruits and vegetables, which naturally contains healthy and super-hearty bacteria for your gut. (Out of a genuine need I could see in the market, I created, with much passion, research, and care, an effective SBO probiotics formula containing proper ratios of strains. If you feel drawn, you can check out the Resources section or my website for info.)

- Drink the Power Protein Smoothie. The Propelled Heart can exhibit a lot of lack-thinking, worrying that you are always missing something or that there is a gap. You can put this searching to rest by consuming this daily powerhouse drink which contains so many essential daily nutritional and nourishing needs in its ingredients: protein, chia seeds, greens powder, and whole fruit such as bananas or frozen acai. (You can also find the recipe on my site.) When I started drinking this myself nearly every day, it simplified my overall diet as well as overthinking about my diet. I usually drink the Power Protein Smoothie in the afternoon, and I drink the Glowing Green Smoothie in the morning.

- Make time for massage and self-massage. Ayurveda teaches that working with the skin, which is dense with nerve endings, is a great way to balance your nervous system and bring you into your body and into the present moment. The Propelled Heart can often slip into anxious energy, being up in the head, and overthinking, so soothing your skin and being in the present moment can be a potent antidote to help support more coherence and peace.

- Regularly stretching for 10 or more minutes. Being in one stretch for at least six to eight breaths without actively "doing" anything will help build your "stillness muscle." It's a wonderful practice to allow you to tune more into your breath and into the stillness within us all. Become aware of tight areas in both your body and mind, and focus on softening and breathing through them.

- Drink ginger tea in the evenings. This is a wonderful digestive aid that helps warm your *agni*, or digestive fire, as it helps center you back into yourself as you sip it. It is an aid to help reign in an overactive mind that can lead to burnout at any time, but particularly at the end of the day.

Key Points of the Propelled Heart:
The Beginning of Coherence

- The Propelled Heart is driven into action; driven by the inner struggle to seek meaning and belonging.

- There is more coherence than the last stage, but it's not yet fully harnessed by the heart. As such, at the Propelled Heart stage there is a tendency to overthink, overanalyze, experience restlessness and lack-based thinking, and chase externals (material objects, titles, labels, an increasingly "better" body) to feel enough.

- Unlocking more of your heart's power allows you to feel your wholeness, which is the key to finding inner peace and easefully creating more abundance.

- The Heart-Gut Alignment Practice can help you access the wisdom of your two other "brains"—your heart and your gut—to create more clarity and creativity, and to make the best decisions across your life.

- Harmony is the ultimate form of stress resilience, by learning to pivot and flow with life instead of resisting and going into a stress response.

- The HeartAlign Harmonize Method is an on-the-spot technique that you can practice right in the midst of your life in as little as *one minute* to help you access the power of your heart, avoid stress and negativity, and create harmony and coherence.

The amazing energy of the Propelled Heart deepens into greater coherence over time. You feel a growing stabilization in your day-to-day moments rising up from within your own heart, which steadies you through life's ups and downs. You start to become your own anchor in life.

You begin to transition to the next heart stage, which is the Steady Heart. More emotional balance, peace, and coherence await!

Let's keep going in our heart journey. . . .

Chapter 5

STAGE 3

THE STEADY HEART: COHERENCE AND CONNECTION

As we enter the Steady Heart, something extraordinary happens. We reach a turning point in our heart journey, for this is the first stage where the heart starts to lead our life more than our ego.

Sri Yukteswar teaches that the core essentials of life are *sat* (existence), *chit* (consciousness), and *nanda* (bliss): "These three are the real necessities of the human heart and have nothing to do with anything outside his Self."[46] The Steady Heart arises as we embody the kind of self-reliance that Sri Yukteswar speaks of our basic physical needs, all that we actually need coming from within us. There is a steady anchor in our heart we can align ourself with throughout life, regardless of what is occurring in the outside world.

Our heart then becomes a steady source for all that we used to think depended on the outside world: security, confidence, love, fulfillment, peace, and, over time as we continue to awaken our hearts, the unfolding of true bliss. Our steady heart brings us back home to ourselves, to experience the essential power of who we really are on a moment-to-moment basis.

Our heart becomes a shore. Imagine a solid, safe haven from a rocking ocean. An eternal shore that is the solace from the waves of life. This is where we find our True Self. This is where we find the strength and power to overcome any obstacle or issue that life brings our way. This is where we discover the peace that passes all understanding.

Life brings us many waves, big ones and small ones that can occur multiple times a day. Steadiness requires an awareness of when we have left the shore—the steadiness of the heart—and have become *unsteady* by getting tossed around in the waves of the ocean. This means the times when we overidentify with the thoughts, feelings, and physical sensations that arise. The unsteady heart gets itself into trouble, because it believes all that the wild horse mind is saying. When the waves of big thoughts and feelings rise up, including old wounds from the past that create reactions in the present, we become aware that incoherence—unsteadiness—is coming in, and we simply relax our body and mind and let all the sensations wash over us, like moving through a waterfall.

The priority lies in *going to the heart.* That is the only thing on the to-do list in those moments! It's essential to refrain from speaking, deciding, or acting while we are in the middle of being tossed in a surge of thoughts, feelings, and sensations. By avoiding getting entangled in the ego's maze of narratives and stories, we maintain our center. As strong as the thoughts and sensations can all feel in the moment, it will all pass. Let it. It's like getting off the roller coaster at the end of the ride. It felt wild for a few minutes, but we get right back to where we started the ride, intact!

Calmness and coherence return once you sit on the steady shore of your heart. Then your heart's enormously powerful wisdom rises up to show you the way forward—wisdom that is in alignment with your values and who you are. When you act on your heart's wisdom instead of from a reactionary place, you can feel good about yourself and how you are handling life. In his essay *Self-Reliance*, Ralph Waldo Emerson says, "Nothing can bring you peace but yourself."[47]

As you start to find your way back and discover the power of your heart and who you really are, you can also help others discover their brilliant hearts too.

UNLOCKING EMOTIONAL INTELLIGENCE FOR GREATER SUCCESS

Managing your emotions to create emotional self-mastery, known as emotional intelligence, will allow you to have better daily experiences and create more success. This is because emotional intelligence improves how you communicate, express your needs, and have them met, while feeling in unity with others and the world.

Emotional intelligence comes into play at the Steady Heart stage because, as you find the steady anchor of your heart, you create more emotional mastery. Your growing heart intelligence is the basis of emotional intelligence. Your emotions don't have to run the show anymore, and you don't have to feel that you are at the mercy of big emotions or feelings.

The holistic wellness philosophy I teach within my brand Solluna centers on Four Cornerstones: Food, Body, Emotional Well-being and Spiritual Growth. The Emotional Well-being Cornerstone has been the most personally challenging for me of all the Cornerstones. I didn't have tools for dealing with big, overwhelming feelings and things I witnessed around me as I child, so I shut down and buried the feelings. And part of myself. Later on, these big energies, these traumas still very much there and lodged in my body, would create emotional swings, sometimes when least expected.

I had so much stored pain around not being enough that if something touched it, like someone making some comments that made me feel that they did not seem to understand me or see me in the way I wanted to be seen, I would get deeply triggered and fly off the handle. Even if I seemed like my normal self on the outside, inside I would be seething, like a smoldering volcano. Sometimes I would develop a dislike or resentment toward that person, an aversion to being around them or inviting them to events or going to the same places as them. It was all a way to feel safe, but as you can imagine, it made my world smaller and smaller. It was my husband, Jon, who bravely brought forward to me, "How come you let that person bother you so much? Who cares?"

For over a decade, my best friend, John, has been a patient listener for countless hours over the phone, talking to me about those feelings of trigger in order to make me feel okay and safe. Over time, I stopped needing to talk to an outside person so much and so often in order to feel soothed and okay. I started to become more in touch with the energies moving through my body, within me, and to see that emotions really are just energy, and that I had the strength and the developing vision to see beyond the stories. I could see that I didn't have to buy into all the mind's thoughts as "truth." The HeartAlign Steady in Life Practice is a practice that I use all the time, sometimes multiple times a day. I can say with much gratitude that this heart work really works, and it does get easier and easier.

So what exactly is emotional intelligence? Emotional intelligence was brought into the mainstream in 1995 with Daniel Goleman's groundbreaking book *Emotional Intelligence*. In this book, Goleman offered cutting-edge research confirming that success in life is based more on your ability to manage your emotions than your intellectual capabilities. Goleman's research explains why individuals with a high IQ in life can experience a lack of success. And yet those with a moderate IQ but higher emotional awareness who apply insight of that awareness to daily life, known as *emotional intelligence*, can create exceptional success in their professional and personal lives. According to research, unlike IQ, emotional intelligence (EQ) can be developed and increased throughout your life.

You don't have to be a genius to be happy and successful, although you do have to learn to self-manage your own emotions. This requires some effort to shift your patterns, but you can definitely do so from your all-powerful heart. Heart intelligence is the foundation of emotional intelligence. It's not linear, and it's not about thinking your way through. Positive thinking can feel forced and inauthentic, and it often fails to alter your mood. That is because your mind can know the "right" thoughts but still not follow them. It can be very stubborn! Our nerve cells actually retain and store accumulated memories from the past with the emotional charge assigned to them.[48] That means that pain, trauma, and memories are actually stored inside of us and can hijack our thoughts in the present moment.

Focusing on self-generating, positive, heart-centered *feelings* or *positive heart emotions* at will, such as compassion, care, appreciation, and love is a core way to elevate your emotional intelligence. That's because the more you are in these feelings, the more you have the power to shift your mood, change your life experience, and trans- form the thoughts you are thinking. *So it's always more powerful to go to the heart and work with the heart emotions first, which will then shift your thoughts.*

You learned how to self-generate positive heart feelings and emotions with the HeartAlign Meditation and other practices offered throughout this book, which focus on appreciation and then can naturally expand into care, love, or the other heart emotions. The more you regularly practice these tools, the more these positive heart emotions become your regular state of being. You can then expand your emotional intelligence to create incredible relation- ships and effective communication, which will begin to create amazing harmony and success in your home and professional life.

EMOTIONS ARE ENERGY—AND ENERGY CAN BE NEUTRAL

Emotions are merely forms of energy. The word *emotion* derives from the Latin verb "to move" and literally means "energy in motion." Feelings are sensations, and so emotions are strong feelings, such as love and anger, that move you. They literally move energy through your body. Emotions create powerful changes in your body, mind, and nervous system.

Today, there is confusion around the notion that freely wielding your ideas, feelings, and opinions is a part of self- expression. Some believe having big outbursts of anger or other strong emotions is healthy. Sigmund Freud advocated for this early on, which he said would promote an emotional clearing. Later he discontinued this practice.

Science now shows us that these big blowouts of emotional expression are *not* healthy. They are damaging to your system. Research conducted by Aron Siegman at the University of Maryland found that people who reacted with impulsive outbursts of anger proved to be at a higher risk for coronary heart disease than those who kept their anger inside.[49] Negative emotions create illness and accelerated aging—which none of us want.

Today, psychologists have come to realize that expressing anger and hurt feelings doesn't make them go away. It can actually reinforce the emotional pattern in the brain's neural circuitry. This means the more you talk about it and bring up angry emotions, the more you keep the anger alive, and the more those stressful and highly charged emotional thoughts harm your body.[50] So the more you complain to others about how your friend didn't show up for you the way you wanted her to, the more you remain angry. Can you relate to a time when you just got more and more mad, the more you kept thinking about and telling the story about how you were wronged?

This doesn't mean that it's healthy to suppress emotions either. You don't want emotions to build up inside you. The key is to recognize the big feelings are there and then learn the heart intelligent way of digesting them first so that you can respond to whatever life brings you in the best ways and not just in old patterns.

It means that a big part of emotional intelligence is shifting and holding your attention *within yourself.* When triggered or upset, focus on relaxing and calming down your body and mind so that your own heart intelligence has the space to create coherence within you. Move your attention away from believing all the thoughts or focusing on what other people did or said. This is where real self-reliance—and real personal power—builds.

We have grown so accustomed to reacting to our wild horse mind and all the wild thoughts it feeds us. When we feel the pain of the past, we subconsciously say "ouch!" like we touched a hot stove. We then instantly jump to, "I don't want to feel that again. Let's not go there." Then the pain gets projected out, either in anger or frustration, or in trying to "do" something to feel better or numb the pain, whether that is putting our heads down and working, drinking, turning on a show, or whatever is our go-to tool. And the pain stays there, waiting to be triggered again until we actually process it and clear it out, once and for all.

The heart says, "Hold on here. I don't want to live this triggered existence. I want to be free." It doesn't want to protect itself with the armor of harsh emotions like anger or a false sense of superiority. It values freedom over the familiar. Freedom comes from being steady in the heart and not tossed around by life and other people, none of which we can control.

While feelings and sensations can feel strong, they can also be neutral. It's the *thoughts* you have about certain emotions and the reactions and patterns in your body that make emotions register as negative or positive to you. Thoughts create the resistance to the triggers. That's why it has felt so difficult to shift behaviors until now. Rehashing old memories often reinforces the memories in the cells of the brain, instead of creating a way to process the memories to release them. The same old memories keep the hurt and the ego's justification to hold on to the grudge or the resentment alive. The mind alone will never free you.

What *will* free you is your heart. Research has found that as your coherence increases, so too does the two-way communication system happening between your heart and your brain.[51] As your heart intelligence turns on, you start to feel differently in your moment-to-moment experience. You will be freer in the present, consciousness will grow, and so will bliss.

Digesting life through your heart can save you years spent attempting to understand and process past or present experiences solely through talk therapy or analyzing from a mental place. While talk therapy can have great benefits, it may have limitations, especially if it continues to reinforce linear thinking. Such thinking can perpetuate deep-rooted patterns and feelings of blame, victimhood, lack, and scarcity.

Your heart is so strong. Your heart holds your greatest power at the core of who you really are, a power that surpasses any limited pattern or negative emotion that keeps surfacing. Your Steady Heart *can* hold strong, hold the space for coherence, as well as for the incoherent sensations to wash over you, and encourage your power and wisdom to rise up in your life.

The HeartAlign Steady in Life Practice

The Steady in Life Practice is designed to allow you to feel the steadiness of your heart, a place you can return to throughout your day. It can help you be more resilient against the stress responses caused by thoughts, feelings, and physical sensations.

The HeartAlign Harmonize Method discussed in the Propelled Heart chapter (Chapter 4) is a tool to support you in creating more harmonious action steps and solutions in your day-to-day life, when triggered. The Steady in Life Practice, on the other hand, is designed to help you shift into being more anchored in your heart on a moment-to-moment basis, so that your reality shifts into a more heart-centered existence in general!

The more nonreactive we become to life, the calmer we are, and the more our heart's intelligence can center—and lead—our lives. Laura Pringle, an intuitive coach who helps people heal their trauma and ingrained reactions, notes, "The heart knows that the mind can make many complicated realities from 'actuality.' When your mind complicates things, let your heart call you back to what IS."[52]

You can also find great solace in realizing that you have a portable sanctuary inside of you. When life feels like it's flowing, you can fully enjoy the moment by being in your heart, awake, present, and confident from feeling a steady connection to your own inner heart's light. And when things feel rocky or chaotic, you can retreat to the safe space of your heart.

You begin to feel an easygoing, powerful sense of being ever-centered in your heart, and you feel more bliss, confidence, and peace across all your life.

Here are the steps of the Steady in Life Practice:

1. Keep a steady awareness on your heart as you move through your day.

2. When you start to feel unsteady from thoughts, feelings, and physical sensations, take slow, deep breaths and let them wash over you while you stay connected to your heart.

3. Return to a calm, coherent state in your heart
    before you take action, speak, or proceed in
    any way.

Here is a more detailed explanation to the steps:

1. **Keep a steady awareness on your heart as you
    move through your day.** You can feel connected
    to your heart as your center, an inner anchor that
    is always there as you move through your day. You
    don't have to place your full awareness on your
    heart, as we do in the HeartAlign Meditation, but
    part of your awareness can always be focused on
    your heart. Notice how this awareness gives you
    great energy and a sense of dependable comfort
    and steadiness, all from inside of you.

2. **When you start to feel unsteady from thoughts,
    feelings, and physical sensations, take slow,
    deep breaths and let them wash over you while
    you stay connected to your heart.** Stay aware
    when strong thoughts, feelings, and sensations
    attempt to pull you out of your heart. Remember
    that overidentifying with these things is exactly
    what makes us unsteady! We are *not* our thoughts,
    feelings, and physical sensations. They are
    energies that come and go like waves. You want
    to make space for the feelings and not push them
    away or down or disassociate from them if they are
    there anyways. Notice them, feel them, and allow
    them to pass through, without creating a story or
    narrative around them such as, *I shouldn't have
    to feel this,* or *She is the problem and is making
    me feel this way!* Remind yourself that it's all just
    energy moving through.

    Focus on relaxing your body and your mind. Allow
    your shoulders to relax down if they became
    hunched up, and relax any clenching in your belly
    or throughout your body. Imagine you are taking
    deep breaths in and out of your heart, slow and
    steady coherence-building breaths.

If you take your attention away from the thoughts and sensations and really focus your awareness on your heart and your breath, you will usually return to calmness in a few moments (if you find yourself struggling with some deeper trauma that keeps coming into your life, please do seek professional counseling as well).

Don't rush the process. Let your heart show you the way back.

3. **Return to a calm, coherent state in your heart before you take action, speak, or proceed in any way.** When the strong energies subside, you will feel a deep, peaceful calm like after a storm. Your Steady Heart is what carried you safely through the storm!

After the storm, after the reactivity of the big waves, notice the deep peace, the higher awareness that follows. You're now in a position to make clear, wise decisions, from an emotionally intelligent, coherent way going forward that you can feel really proud of and that aligns with your values.

This practice is very powerful—and practical—in helping to break habitual reactions and addictive, old patterns like over-eating, or reaching for the regular soothing aids, whether it be wine, weed, zoning out to excessive screen watching, or whatever has helped you to quell the uncomfortable emotions and sensations that rise up.

A client, Riley, we will call her, would often get extremely triggered with overwhelming feelings when she went on social media and at social events. She would slip into comparing or judging people she came across or finding ways to put them down, and she felt like she was in constant competition with others. This all came from a place of her nervous system registering a sense of threat. And these threat-based thoughts greatly drained her energy. They also created a lot of ups and downs in her day—and she would often reach for sugary treats or more coffee, which ultimately made her feel more depleted and frustrated.

We did a social media detox for a while, while she worked on connecting to her heart more and doing the HeartAlign Meditation each morning as her foundation. She also focused on eating more regular meals and going to bed and waking up at the same times, which also created regularity in her life. When she did get back into social media (which was a part of her job and unavoidable), she used the HeartAlign Steady in Life Practice and felt more and more equipped to handle the swells of big sensations, "stay in her own lane of focus" as she puts it, and not feel so thrown off. Today, she continues to do this practice and work, and is far more calm and centered. Comparison and judgment in her life, by her estimate, are down by about 80 percent.

ATTACHMENTS TRANSFORM
INTO GREATER LOVE

When my first baby was born, I couldn't believe the intensity of the love that came along with this tiny, cuddly bundle. It was a purity of love unmatched by anything I had ever felt until that point. I was so enraptured with this little creature that he was always on my body, literally attached to me. The parenting style coined "attachment parenting" made me feel that this level of perpetual togetherness was a normalized, excellent path of parenting to follow. And it was, as far as closeness and emotional support.

As he grew, I could see that in some ways we had crossed into unhealthy attachment. Whenever he wasn't napping, I felt the need to play with him and pay attention to him nearly every waking minute. Even though I was running a business and a podcast (which I only shot during his nap times) and was writing books as well, I refused to get any regular help watching him. This created depletion and exhaustion in me. I had to work all hours of the night to get my work and writing done.

Over time, I had a profound and surprising realization from my heart: this was really not about my son at all. I realized when I really looked inward and reflected deeply, that this was really about abandonment trauma that, until then, I was unaware I'd been holding my entire life. My mother had "left me" to go back to work when I was only two weeks old. And this left a deep imprint somewhere deep down in my heart. This kind of clinging, holding my little boy so closely at all times, was a manifestation of that unhealed wound. It was my mind's way of trying to hold on to the love to keep it safe, since it felt so precious.

And that was also why, I further realized, I had often chosen "safe" romantic relationships, where I knew the other person wouldn't leave me. It would be me who would leave, or could then control doing the abandoning. All this was suddenly in plain sight, coming up to be healed, as I became more anchored in my Steady Heart. From my Dark Heart perspective, I couldn't see it at all.

Wow. These were big, painful realizations to take in. It was hard to see and accept, and I went through feelings of grief so intense I felt like my heart was being ripped out. I had to actually face and process the original pain of abandonment through my early childhood, which I had never done before. I started doing the HeartAlign Steady in Life Practice as the feelings of attachment would rear up, and I began to be there for myself to move through them. And each time I did, I felt a little stronger. Eventually, I found steady love inside of my own heart. A love not dependent on any other.

I began to experience the truth for myself of what Sri Yukteswar taught when he said that all the necessities of our heart are found *within* our heart. Things became balanced. My son and I have actually become even closer and more deeply connected, because now there is more freedom in our relationship without the unhealthy overintensity. My son not only taught me how much I could love another human, but our relationship also helped guide me back to find the true source of love within my own heart.

Healing attachment in this one huge way created a greater unlocking across my heart that opened up my whole life to far more love. It paved the path for me to unite with my husband. The love between us was so massive, I couldn't control it. So previously I would have probably run away from it because it wouldn't have registered as safe enough. I am so grateful that we really can heal these blocks in our heart. And I am so excited for *you* to do the same. Look into any patterns in your life that you now realize may not be super healthy. You can start to shift them now!

In order to truly love others, you must be free of them. That means free of needing them to love you back, favor you, see you, understand you, agree with you, validate you, or have favorable opinions of you. Love is free and freeing. Real love does not expect anything in return, though attachments do.

The source of love is inside of your own heart. The more you deepen into the Steady Heart, the more this truth will come forward. Once you find that the source of love is inside of yourself, you can love others even more fully, with no expectation in return and without distortion.

And while it feels wonderful to love others and share life with loved ones, they are still not the source of love. It can be a journey to realize this, as it was for me, and that is okay too. Let your heart teach you the truth. Real love does not deplete. That is why when you free yourself from needing the love of others, you can actually love them more and become closer to them in a genuine way. Love will grow and thrive.

STEADY LOVE BEYOND ATTACHMENTS AND AVERSIONS

Spiritual traditions teach us that in order to ascend to higher consciousness and open our heart more, we have to heal attachments and aversions. Attachments are when we thirst after objects or people *outside* of us to try to fulfill happiness. Attachments mean we misplace love and our power externally. Because attachments are a clingy, sticky energy that is not coherent or free, they lead to the disharmonious energies of fear, frustration, infatuation, obsession, anger, possessiveness, and jealousy.

Attachments also include strong desires for material objects or experiences. It's the feeling of "I must have" that certain apartment, the designer purse, the perfect golf clubs, the reservation to the show, the exact vacation. Desire is a never-ending energy field. Yogananda teaches us, "The thing is this: it is not wrong to have possessions, but it is wrong to be possessed by possessions. You must be free from attachment."[53]

Aversions are another issue. They create fear in your life because they reinforce the limited belief that certain situations or conditions can take love away from you or have the power to make you unhappy. If you have a strong aversion to not being in a relationship, you believe that if you're single you will be unhappy and lack love. Or, you might create an aversion to a relative or co-worker, so that when you're around that person, you give them the power to make you feel annoyed or to close your heart.

Attachment and aversion take you out of the Steady Heart. They make you feel unsteady instead, because they are rooted in the mistaken belief that love has to be sought outside of yourself and can be taken away.

The Steady Heart discovers more and more freedom. It realizes that the love, happiness, and approval it previously misplaced outside of itself can be found within itself.

Nonattachment allows you to remain clear. And clarity can express as love and other heart qualities. Nonattachment isn't cold. It means your sense of love is safely held within, instead of always looking to suction its sense of love from others, like an octopus. Then you can create something really healthy: connection. Connection allows you to be fully loving and free to be yourself with others, and they can be free to be themselves with you too.

In order to heal your attachments and aversions so you can be free, you first have to become aware of them. The feelings of attachment and aversion are definitely unsteady, because they are not of the heart. They create a sense of tightness or constriction, tinged with the desperate energy of "it must be this way," which feels very different from the expansive feeling of being in your heart.

The triggering of attachments and aversions can arise in large and small ways in daily life. Become aware of these situations. These can include your favorite café being closed that day, a tech malfunction that keeps you from watching your favorite show, pain from a child growing up or leaving for college or not needing you in the same ways anymore, or the disappointment of not receiving texts back from your love interest. Perhaps it's the ache of a relationship or vacation ending or having to move away from your beloved apartment or home.

As you become aware that unsteadiness is arising from an attachment or an aversion, just like handling other strong feelings, go into the HeartAlign Steady in Life Practice on the spot. That is, shift your awareness into your heart, take some deep breaths, and allow the sensations of attachment or aversion to pass through.

As you do this, you will bring your heart's powerful coherence to the incoherent, needy feelings of attachment or aversion. Let them wash over and subside, whether that takes a few seconds or minutes. It may come up a few—or many times—around the same situation, and that's okay! Keep reminding yourself it's just energy, and as long as you let it pass through instead of buying into any stories your wild horse mind may be trying to tell you, it's all just going to subside. Then you can regain your centeredness and clarity, and you can trust yourself to speak and act, once you've settled down!

As you anchor more deeply back into the Steady Heart, let it teach you the truth: *You do not need to try to hold on to anything.* Love is inside and cannot be taken away from you. You are okay, no matter what shifts or changes, no matter what comes or doesn't come. There is great power in allowing things to come and go as they will and know that the steadiness, the peaceful stillness in you is a constant.

My client Franklin, as we will call him, was well-known in his industry and had a long-term weight problem. He overate to deal with his feelings and was extremely sensitive about what others thought of him. Once, when a project didn't go as well as he wanted it to, he felt so embarrassed that he moved across the country for a while! During this time, his weight further ballooned.

My work to help get Franklin healthier and reset his portion sizes wasn't possible until he was able to move past relying on food as his emotional aid. Like many of us, he had never been taught how to feel feelings and sensations and simply let them pass through him. We agreed that he would do the HeartAlign Steady in Life Practice and set a timer for at least 30 minutes before eating anything, to see if he really did need the food. Over time, he lost over 50 pounds—and kept it off. He was amazed to see that sensations come and go, and he really didn't have to stuff them down with food!

Signs of Attachment and Aversion

- Needy
- Pushy
- Overly emotional
- Frantic
- Desperate
- Jealous
- Craving
- Addiction
- Overemphasizing "special"
- Envy
- Vindictive
- Clingy

Signs of Connection

- Calm
- Peaceful
- Accepting of others' needs, opinions, and independence
- Centered in the heart
- Nonattached, allowing for healthy time apart
- Being and allowing freedom
- Content
- Harmonious

STEADYING YOURSELF AROUND CHALLENGING PEOPLE

Sri Yukteswar teaches us that awakening and opening our heart further requires "evenmindedness in all conditions."[54] And let's face it: some of the most challenging conditions we ever have to face and learn to grow beyond include other people.

It's easy to drop into old patterns, to keep the same sense of blame or separation you feel with others. *Well, she did this,* or *He did that to me, and it just isn't right.* And yet, even if people remain as they are around you, your heart can help you change your attitude toward them and allow you to see things in a completely different way than you ever dreamed was possible.

When you have a certain attitude, and maintain it over time, your brain literally rewires itself to facilitate that attitude.[55] So this is why you might have certain feelings toward certain people, why they may annoy you or trigger you so much. It's because of something that happened long ago that got stored in your body, even if you don't even consciously remember what it was exactly. The good news is that attitudes can shift and be rewired, which can lead to balance and steadiness! And more freedom. If people annoy us, they have a sort of power over us. The power to rob us of peace and steadiness, which is a power we do not want to give away.

Yogananda said, "From the moment you set foot on the spiritual path, nothing happens by coincidence."[56] We can expand the definition of spiritual path to simply mean a path of growth. The higher intelligence that weaves the whole universe together places people in your path to help you grow past limitations in your own character. In this way, you can start to see that everything—and everyone!—is a gift sent to help you become stronger and move back into the True Self.

When someone is brought to your doorstep who is challenging for you—a mother-in-law, a colleague at work, a friend of a friend, or whoever—turn the spotlight of awareness back to the Steady Heart within you. Ask yourself, what can I learn from this person or situation? How can I become more resilient within my own heart?

Personal power grows when you don't give your very power away by allowing someone to take your peace or happiness. Your peace is not up for grabs when it's rooted in the unshakable place of the Steady Heart center.

Molly, as we will call her, joined my Solluna team and came in a bit hot and rough around the edges with her communication. We hired her because she had great ideas and a lot of enthusiasm, and she was really great at her job. However, she triggered me because she often got so excited that she interrupted me, was really talkative, and quite abrupt when she disagreed with something.

We could have gone with someone easier, but I went into my heart and felt strongly that she was a gift given to me, not just in her work skills but also as a challenge to stretch me to stay more steady in myself. I found a way to guide some communication boundaries without clipping her wings. There's still some bumps here and there, but I focus on continually seeing her big heart and sincere intentions when she does annoy me. It helps me to take a breath and get myself more coherent before responding! We have both grown in this relationship, and the work thrives.

Here are some practical tips for growing in situations with people you find challenging:

- Stay in your heart. Focus on becoming more coherent and sending out positive heart emotions or at least neutrality.

- Be self-aware if you do get triggered by another person. Come right into your HeartAlign Steady in Life Practice as soon as you feel it.

- While you are in a conversation or an interaction with someone you find challenging, concentrate on locating a place of connection. That is, pinpoint something you can appreciate about that person. If you really look, you will find something.

- If you find yourself around someone complaining, being negative, or coming from a limited perspective, try to zoom out of the situation, as if you were watching it objectively from a distance. Instead of getting entangled in it and feeling pulled down, shift into feeling compassion and extra kindness for where that person is struggling, or at least get to a more neutral place. See it from your heart's wisdom.

- Instead of trying to convince someone or getting defensive, which is energy-depleting and futile, choose brief, nonengaging statements like, "Maybe you're right" or "Time will tell." You're not agreeing with them; you're taking the neutral path of creating a strong boundary with your energy by not engaging.

- Create healthy boundaries. Just because you have an open heart doesn't mean that everyone gets full access to you. If someone causes harm, it's really important to be discerning and establish clear boundaries about where that person can and can't come into your life. This is important and a healthy part of self-care and preserving your own well-being.

You will see that over time even the most challenging people do not have to affect you. Your heart center becomes increasingly imperturbable and impenetrable. And that level of strength and inner peace is priceless.

Nightly Reflection

Yogananda said that "True self-analysis is the greatest art of progress."[57] Constantly tuning inward and analyzing yourself allows your heart to keep opening and growing in more power and light.

If you want to be a heart-centered person, you must decide that for yourself and then live it, willing yourself to be heart-centered in your daily life. That means you continue aligning more and more with your heart's intelligent guidance. Sometimes you listen to it, sometimes you don't, and it's okay. Because in creating daily and honest awareness of yourself, you can keep working to align your actions with your heart, and ultimately find a way to success.

Here are three questions you can consider or journal about in the evenings, as you reflect on the day:

- How closely did I align with my heart today?

- What could I have done differently by applying more heart intelligence?

- What did I learn?

HEART EMBODIMENT:
Lifestyle Tips to Support and Deepen into the Steady Heart

The following lifestyle tips can further support your deepening into the anchor of your Steady Heart:

- **Create regular routines:** In Ayurveda this is known as *dinacharya*, or daily routine. It's believed that more regularity in your daily activities promotes deeper self-care, modulating your biological clock to be more in tune with the rhythms of nature, and bringing more self-awareness, all of which will ultimately make you more steady in your body and foster more steadiness in your heart. As such, make an effort to eat meals at regular times as well as exercise, go to bed, and wake up around the same times. This will help to promote better digestion, better sleep, and higher energy, all of which contribute to more heart connection and coherence.

- **Increase your fiber intake:** Fiber is a natural way to feel more full and steady physically, without being overly heavy or dense. It's a natural way to create healthy portion sizes without having to obsess over numbers or count calories, allowing for more natural self-regulation. Only plant foods contain fiber, so be sure to load up on veggies and salads, and try incorporating the amazingly energizing Glowing Green Smoothie in your mornings (see the Resources section or my site if you feel drawn to making it for yourself!).

- **Incorporate backbends:** Yoga *asanas*, or poses, that are backbends are said to help open the energy of the *anahata* heart chakra. A central theme in this book is that the heart is both physical and energetic, and you want to work on both levels to open it! Start with gentle ones, like simply holding the sides of your chair as you stay seated, and gently leaning back and lifting your chin a few inches.

- **Gentle sunbathing:** In the Vedas, considered the oldest scriptures in the world, the sun is an important symbol of light. The brilliant power of the sun supports all life on the planet, including plants, animals, and humans. It can also help connect you to the energy of the brilliant power of your own heart. And vitamin D, absorbed into the body from sunlight, has been shown to benefit cardiac health.

  I say *gentle* to mean sitting in the early morning or late afternoon sunlight if possible, using adequate sun protection for your skin type (I always cover my face and neck with a hat and only get the sunlight on my limbs), and only for about 10 to 15 minutes. You can start with just two minutes and work up to a few more. You can also try doing the HeartAlign Meditation or the Experiencing Your Abundant Wholeness Practice discussed in the Propelled Heart chapter (Chapter 4), in the beautiful, enlivening sunshine.

- **Balance your macronutrients of fat, protein, and carbs:** Steadiness and balance require tuning in to your unique energetic blueprint, your constitution, and eating accordingly for that particular season, day, or time of your life. For instance, in the cold winter you may naturally be drawn to more fat, like heartier coconut-lentil and other soups, stews, and meals. In the summer you may find yourself naturally craving lighter salad meals and raw fruit. There are times you naturally need more strengthening protein. Your body and your needs are unique, so please don't just base how you eat on some rigid diet or what someone else is eating! Tune in to your heart and gut to best care for your own vitality.

Key Points of the Steady Heart:
Coherence and Connection

- In the Steady Heart there is the realization that your center is within and you can be stable and steady no matter what is going on outside of you.

- Heart coherence greatly grows in this stage, as there is more entrainment, or harmony, between the heart, brain, and nervous system.

- Emotional intelligence expands as your heart's awakening brilliant intelligence allows you to experience more positive heart emotions, more easily shift negative thinking and perspectives, and balance the erratic emotions of the ego.

- The HeartAlign Steady in Life Practice allows you to be more anchored in your heart through life's many ups and downs, and remain more centered, even as strong feelings and sensations, and fearful or negative thoughts arise.

- In order to keep unlocking your heart, it's necessary to shed attachments and aversions, which are ultimately lack-based, and realize that the wholeness within you can never be diminished.

The growing sturdiness and centeredness of the Steady Heart allows for the next stage of your heart to be unlocked, and once again there is going to be a *huge* shift.

What unfolds next, in the Devoted Heart stage, includes you accessing a high level of intuition. In a way, it will be like putting on special glasses to enable you to see much, much more in any given situation. Your awakening heart will give you a whole new vision of the world.

And you are going to start to harness the real power of love. Not in a sentimental way, but in an incredibly intelligent way that unites, finds solutions, and forges the best way forward that is as peaceful as it is powerful.

Let's start unlocking Stage 4: The Devoted Heart!

Chapter 6

STAGE 4

THE DEVOTED HEART:
INTUITION AND
FORGIVENESS

Devotion is a focused commitment to something, with constancy, loyalty, and attentiveness.

At the Devoted Heart stage, there is such a high level of heart awakening that you become *devoted* to the heart. You become devoted and faithful to the heart and its innate energy and qualities, such as peace, love, and compassion.

At this stage, you don't just feel your heart as your center, which you discovered in the Steady Heart—your whole life becomes more oriented, or as Sri Yuketswar says, "devoted"[58] to the inner world rather than the outer world.

You realize that your life works *so* much better when your heart is leading the way, and you surrender to its profound wisdom and intelligence time and time again. Life then opens up in extraordinary ways of ease and abundance that previously didn't even seem possible.

So much of my Devoted Heart has opened up through family life. There are so many pathways that spur our heart's awakening, and for me a big one is the love of my family.

When my husband and I met, our love was powerful, as I've shared with you. But there was also a lot of turbulence in those first few years. My safety triggers went down enough to allow the marriage, but then they flared back up, a hundred times stronger, after we were married. There were many times I pulled away in a passive-aggressive way when I didn't feel safe because I didn't feel I was seen or heard in the way I wanted to be by him, and vice versa. We are both strong. Each of us could dig into our stories and be stubborn that we were "right."

At some point, I looked at my kids' beautiful faces, and at my beloved husband, and realized that I was going to be Devoted. Devoted to love, to a loving family life, to creating a loving environment for those kids and for all of us. I was going to do what it would take. And let me tell you, I went into my heart and there was a lot to see that was unpleasant.

I had to accept myself first. Within the family life, I could not run away or pretend my shadows weren't there in a shield of contrived perfectionism in other areas, like eating a great diet. I had to accept that I had a lot of unhealed wounds and trauma. I was not broken, and I was still whole, like all of us. But I was in need of some healing. This healing had to take place through my heart, the only place where true acceptance could be found- and also true forgiveness.

I had to forgive myself for all the mean things I said, the people I hurt, the times I lashed out at my husband and others close to me because I was in pain and didn't know how to make myself feel safe and move through it. I had to forgive my parents for not being there for me emotionally in a way I would have liked, though as my heart continued to awaken I came to transcend forgiveness and instead find deep acceptance and the perfection of it all. My childhood and exactly how I was raised really was a perfect gift created specifically for my growth in this lifetime, and I wouldn't trade it for anything.

It's true that not all of this heart work feels so good in the moment. Things will come up for you that are painful and simply hurt. Yet we can make the powerful mindset shift away from victim perspective to seeing *all* the experiences you went through as gifts. And to see that whatever is now coming up can allow a deeper healing, and it can be a pathway for allowing you to access your wholeness and awaken your heart to a whole new level. All your power and beauty is there for you to claim. You don't have to be afraid, because you have your heart to not only guide you through, but also completely be there for you.

A DIFFERENT PRIORITY

It becomes obvious from this level of heart opening that there is no set point to get to in life. Life is not a race to be won. Life is not about ticking things off a list. Someone's gain is not your loss. The means do not justify the ends. There's no prize to win. All the chasing and achievements and gains are not the most important things in life after all. As the old life orientation falls away, a new direction to guide all of life emerges.

That direction for life becomes heart-based living, moment to moment. Living from the heart means living in real abundance. You recognize that all that you were looking for was not only right here but it's here in spades— fulfillment, compassion, peacefulness, appreciation, unity, and, most of all, love. As you live more from your heart in each moment, which is a marker of this stage, you become an embodiment of all these things. And you come to see that abundance, not scarcity, is the real truth of the world.

You can still care about creating success in your career, fun experiences, financial wealth, or a better living situation, but something else has taken greater precedence. This greater priority has transcended all these things and at the same time amplifies *all* of them, since its power is unmatched.

The priority is harmony and love, and everything falls in line behind. In this way, life greatly simplifies. But because the focus on love is primary, you have coherence across your life. *You and the field around you are literally in a higher vibration, and you are actually able to more easily create what you want on a material level.* Good, even incredible circumstances, helpful people, and beneficial situations tend to flow into your life much more.

For instance, I would never have imagined the abundance of nature, in terms of beautiful land, my husband and I would be able to call in to our lives. As my heart unlocked, along with my husband's, and coherence grew in both of us and in our family, blessings also grew around us. We were able to create a permaculture cacao farm in Hawaii, and then double its size in the next year. This was a big contrast to times of the past, including periods where I had to choose between either paying for a yoga class or buying organic cherries, and I lived in a tiny, 400-square-foot apartment that I struggled to pay rent on at times, completely surrounded by concrete in New York City. Such is the power of your awakening heart to change outer circumstances from the inside out. You will also experience this truth more and more as your heart continues to unlock!

Love naturally becomes the predominant energy across your life. Love *is* intelligence in its highest form. It brings unity and harmony, and great abundance as well. You realize a different way to love, one that expands to being nonspecific and not assigned to only certain people and objects. As in, there really is room for everyone. Everyone is a sacred family member. Love becomes your state of being. It becomes the most overwhelmingly important part of your life, and as such, you become Devoted to love.

One Zen proverb points out, "Before enlightenment chop wood, carry water. After enlightenment chop wood, carry water." After reaching high levels of heart intelligence, you still have to go about your daily tasks and responsibilities. Life may look the same in a certain respect, but it will feel radically different because you are experiencing a different level of consciousness at a different level of heart awakening. You now feel expansive, connected, and unified with life to a high degree.

At this stage, it feels foreign when you are *not* in the heart. You find yourself being kind when in the past you might have become angry. You overlook a shortcoming in someone else instead of judging them. You are generous where in earlier heart stages you may have held back. You experience real unconditional love, you feel drawn to serve others, and you embrace forgiveness.

The heart's intelligence is enormous and powerful at this stage, and it's also practical. You know and live the truth that life functions better when you are in your heart. Your intuition increases significantly, and you simply know the best path forward in any given situation. And you also experience enormously better results in your career, your other goals, and your relationships.

The Devoted Heart is incredibly expansive, peaceful, loving, and powerful all at the same time. But keep going, for there are still new levels to tap into.

HEART LANGUAGE CREATES HIGHER INTUITION

Research back in the 1970s by a team at the Fels Research Institute led by physiologists John and Beatrice Lacey discovered that a person's heartbeats weren't just a mechanical pump, but rather formed an *intelligent language.* This intelligent heart language was found to affect the electrical activity of the higher brain centers and significantly influence how a person perceives, reacts, and behaves in the world.[59]

This means that the language of your heart can "speak" to your brain, creating new, higher-level calm responses to life's many happenings. Imagine what life is like for a baby. They cry when they have a need, but the caregiver has to guess which need is being called for. Babies often experience frustration because their lack of language gives them such a limited capacity to express themselves.

Heart intelligence is like adding an important new language into your body—and into your life. A language that is full of deep, intuitive, and expansive information to provide a new level of problem-solving and intelligent guidance. At the Devoted Heart stage, your heart intelligence and the language of your heart greatly awaken to a whole new depth. This higher level of heart language and heart intelligence gives you real freedom in your life, like the baby who starts to feel freer when they are able to speak. No longer stuck in the prison of limited communication, the baby can express when they need milk, when they are tired, or when they need to be changed, and because of this heightened communication, their whole life opens up in an incredible way!

Your heart intelligence helps you become free of the prison you may not have even known you were in, which is old patterns. These patterns include your body entering a stress response from repeated triggers, for example. It also includes patterns of feeling stuck and limited in certain relationships or in work situations. Instead, your heart's power gives you breathing room and the ability to see things from a completely different perspective.

When you engage your heart's power, your internal energy changes in your everyday life. Because you feel differently from within, your behavior also changes. Your work and your relationships will shift as well as the rest of your external life to match up to your altered internal state. Reinstating the language and strengthening the communication of your heart and brain to a whole new level is key to your leading a freer, more happy life.

DEVELOPING YOUR INTUITION

Along the journey from the Dark Heart to this point, you've been working to overcome confusion. Confusion arises when the heart's power is dimmed and can't light the way. Even when you felt more energy at the Propelled Heart stage, you were confused about the best path forward. You may have gone in one direction, then started moving in the opposite direction. You may have picked the wrong partner for personal or business relationships and only in hindsight see all the red flags. You may have been confused about which diet was best for your body or about what to do with your life.

Early on in my business, I created a business partnership with someone I hadn't known for a long period of time. I was excited that he could fill in the technology gaps and other areas I was lacking, and he had a smooth way of talking that made me think he could accomplish so much. I remember not feeling sure if it—if *he*—was right, but I was eager to move ahead to get things going. He ended up stealing quite a bit of money from the business, which created a dramatic end to a partnership that was arduous and unhealthy from the start. Later on, it was quite obvious that my ego was making the decisions, even though my heart had doubts.

At the Devoted Heart stage, much of the prior confusion dissolves. You reach this point, which parallels a high level of heart coherence, through doing the HeartAlign Meditation in Chapter 3 (remember our study participants' coherence increased 29 percent in just one month of practice!), other practices offered in this book, and simply and constantly shifting into your heart and seeking its intelligence to guide you.

This paves the path for intuition. Research reveals that when the heart and brain are in sync and coherence increases, a far deeper intelligence is accessed, and we can then operate at our top performance levels.[60] Most of the authors and entrepreneurs I've interviewed for my *Feel Good* Podcast have mentioned how important intuition was in their success—even in the most tech-heavy of businesses. This deeper intelligence is heart intelligence. And intuition is a core part of heart intelligence.

Higher coherence leads to a calmer, more ordered state throughout your heart rhythms and other systems, which allows you to hear your own intuition. The more coherent you are, the more your intuitive heart can speak to you.

What is intuition, exactly? And how does it speak to us? It's not as tangible and neatly laid out as a typed-up essay, which the wild horse mind would prefer. It's completely beyond the tangible, in fact. Paramahansa Yogananda says of intuition, "It is a deep feeling of *knowing* within you."[61] He also teaches that "It requires no intermediary, no proof from the testimony of the senses or reason."[62] Intuition is not simply based on black-and-white facts or pro-and-con lists. Instead, it involves direct perception. It requires access to deeper intelligence beyond the linear mind, because intuition itself is nonlinear.

Einstein references harmony and alludes to the power of intuition as a feeling when he says:

> "The scientist's religious feeling takes the form of a rapturous amazement at the harmony of natural law, which reveals an intelligence of such superiority that, in comparison with it, all the systematic thinking of human beings is an utterly insignificant reflection. This feeling is the guiding principle of his life and work."[63]

It's exciting to know that your intuition is a superpower that you already have inside of you—you just need to learn to tap into it. Your intuition skyrockets at the Devoted Heart stage, and it will provide you with the best guidance in any decision you have to make in your life. You've probably had the experience of following a hunch, and it led you right. Instead of letting intuition appear randomly, you want to develop it further, in order for your highest success to unfold, which naturally happens in parallel with the rise of heart coherence.

Intuition may arise as feelings, messages, and guidance from within, which is what we have been learning to tune in to more with the HeartAlign practices. It's an intentional looking to heart intelligence for intuitive guidance and allowing space to see what it has to say.

I remember the feeling of talking to my future hubby, Jon, for the first time when met at a Friday night dinner party. While everyone was mingling before dinner, we locked eyes and started tuning in to one another, oblivious to everyone else standing around us. I felt in flow, grounded in my body, and deeply connected to myself and to him. After 15 minutes of chatting, we both suspected we were meant for each other, and it turns out we were.

We went on an early morning beach walk the Saturday morning after the dinner party and decided to attend an event together that same night. In other words, we hung out three separate times in the first 24 hours after we met! And from that day forward, we became nearly inseparable. We were engaged after six weeks, and married less than two weeks after that at the Compton Courthouse, the first available courthouse in Los Angeles we could get into. While in linear time it might seem fast to some, it never did to us or our hearts. Now, years later, we work on our relationship as everyone has to, but our love and connection keeps getting stronger and stronger.

Sometimes intuitive feelings or messages may seem illogical or "wrong" by the linear mind. That's why it's so important to work on increasingly being calmer in your life. Calmness, like clear waters, allows you to listen effectively instead of receiving distorted messages and becoming confused. Calmness keeps you from being tricked by the ego's limited thoughts; chaotic emotions; and old, rigid ideas that can take you down the wrong path.

Furthermore to really turn on your intuition, you must be humble. Why is that? Because humility allows you to remain open and simply accept the best path in any given situation, clear of old, ingrained patterns. It's easy to be stubborn, a quality of the wild horse mind, which finds security in plowing forward in what it thinks it knows is best but actually severely limits your joy and your life. When you are open, amazing paths—and abundance—can astoundingly start to unfold. Notice how the most humble people often create great success.

THE GREATEST FORCE AWAKENS: REAL LOVE

The Devoted Heart realizes a depth of love that was not previously found. Love that is unconditional, unfluctuating, and a permanent state. The spout of love is discovered within your own heart and the truth is revealed: There is no endpoint of love. Love has no limits. It needs no "other" or any sort of object to fulfill its expression. It fulfills itself with its own incredible energy. Because the illusion of lack has been transcended at this stage, the heart is now set up to do what it is meant to do: radiate love.

To be full of love is to be able to give love fully and to also be loveable. The more you love, the more you will receive love. And the more you feel the love within your heart, the more you feel the love inside all other hearts, even if they can't yet feel it for themselves.

The heart can "see" more. Seeing others for who they really are is one of the most powerful acts of love, because it helps them see themselves and find their way back to their own heart. You become a safe person for others, because they can feel that you aren't trying to get something from them. You just love them for who they are.

At previous stages, love is limited to your circle of family and friends. Yet as love expands through the Devoted Heart, it knows no bounds. And so the circle of love grows immensely. It eventually grows to include all. Real love is all-inclusive and rises above preferences. You feel compassion and love for others who pass in front of you at the post office; you care about the person sitting next to you at the restaurant. Even though you don't know them personally, you don't need to. You know they are a member of your family, and you can't exclude them from the halo of your love.

At this stage, love transforms into a reality previously obscured by conditions and limitations. Earlier, love was often tethered to conditions like "I will love you as long as you conform to my desires" or by the expectation that love should be reciprocated in a specific manner, like a two-way street. Instead, love transcends transactional give-and-take status. Love now emanates from your heart unconditionally, without barriers or demands. It's a love that flows freely, without anticipation or reservations.

Unconditional love does not mean we don't need to create healthy boundaries or use our own discernment. You may still naturally gravitate toward some individuals more than others. But without the expectation of receiving love in return, or for it to have to look a certain way, love becomes expansive, all-encompassing, and unrestricted and is offered freely without withholding.

Yogananda said, "Love is the most powerful force that you can have."[64] Most people are in need of the vital soul nutrient of love. When Mother Teresa delivered the commencement address to Harvard graduates in 1982, she said, "Yes there is hunger. Maybe not the hunger for a piece of bread, but there is a terrible hunger for love. We all experience that in our life. The pain, the loneliness."[65] A lack of being in touch with the heart and an inability to feel love is the source of most of the world's problems.

The more you awaken to your Devoted Heart, the more power you have to change the world for the better, starting with the lives of those around you. You have now tapped into the inexhaustible source of love in your energetic heart. And that love is fuel that is very much needed to heal the world. If you look around, you see there is a lot of pain and suffering. There is fear, there is separation, and there are heart blocks that manifest in a million different ways that you can see in the world around you, playing out in the greater collective.

Your heart can heal the root pain and change outcomes. You become a wellspring of love and inspiration for all around you. This includes your family and inner circles and then expands to anyone you happen to be in contact with. It is not an exaggeration to say you really do change lives the more you unlock your heart. This is true in two ways: First, your higher, more coherent electromagnetic heart field helps to create more coherence in the world, without you having to "do" anything. Change starts with you, with your heart, that is. Second, you become a channel for love in action. This means kindness, compassion, love, and care naturally pour out of your actions and words. You simply radiate the power of love, and that shifts and upgrades energy around you, including the energy of others. They may feel differently and change their behaviors just by being around you.

My Auntie Lourdes, who came over from the Philippines and lived with us while growing up, radiated pure love. She was entirely simple; her whole life was work and prayer. She emanated joyful peace and was eternally sweet and loving to me and all who came into her presence. To this day, she remains one of the most magnetic and impactful people I have ever met. That is the kind of love that changes the world.

Spread Love with a Smile

One of the simplest and yet powerful acts of love and service is to smile at someone. A genuine smile from your heart changes the energy around you. It forges an instant connection, a bridge that dispels the illusion that everyone is isolated and separate. A smile reveals the truth of the heart right on your face: *We are in this life together. Let's support each other.*

If someone is having a tough day, a smile can give them newfound energy. It can uplift. If someone is having a great day, a smile can further fuel them. To smile at others is to be generous, to be a "smile millionaire" as Yogananda urges us. Smiling at others is to acknowledge that you have an abundance of love and kindness to give and that you decide to give it, each and every day.

PRACTICAL LOVE IN THE WORLD OF COMMERCE

You can use love practically at work and in business. "But if you guide others with sincere love, you can be a king of hearts,"[66] Yogananda teaches us. Love is not to be misinterpreted as a sentimental, romanticized energy. Businesses constrict when managers and leaders close up their hearts and lead their teams with coldness and rigidity because they think that being rational and practical is the way to create business success. That actually shrinks success because those energies stifle energy and motivation, and so constrain potential.

When you insert love into any business, incredible growth can occur. That's because love is the most expansive, brilliantly intelligent energy. Daniel Lubetzky was so committed to kindness and giving back, that when he founded his company in 2004 he called his brand Kind. He used his company not just to sell bars and snacks, but also as a vehicle to create "the Kind Movement," said to have generated 17+ million everyday acts of kindness. The kind and loving energy at the core of the business also paid off in material profits—as the business was later acquired for $5 billion. Love connects. Love builds. Love grows anything it is added to. Shift your perspective to see where you can love your colleagues and employees, instead of trying to dominate them. People will in turn pour their hearts into their projects and work in a way they never would have been motivated to do, if not for love.

Love your customers and clients, and shift into seeing how you can serve them instead of the other way around. Pour love into creating your products and services from the heart. See how love creates loyalty and natural sharing about your company in a very different way from contrived marketing.

Using force breaks things down, whereas love grows connection and success in any endeavor and any area of your life. Consider when people try to force their way on you or tell you what to do at work. What happens? Probably, you resist, tell them to bug off, or reluctantly give in, but with a tinge of resentment that taints the whole project or task. Either way, force and pushing don't really get you what you want. Yet you would do anything for love. Love gives you energy and motivation. Love is real power.

NEVER MISS AN OPPORTUNITY TO SERVE

As your heart resonance expands, service becomes the primary focus of your life. You will naturally feel called to use your life to benefit others, instead of just the little "me." Your Devoted Heart is so full of love, and love serves, whereas the ego overshadows the heart and seeks to be served in the pursuit of gain. Love looks to give and surrenders wanting something in return, the limits of the "this for that" exchange that occurs at the level of ego.

At the Devoted Heart stage, the self-centered state of mind that had created much tension and discord in the mind and the body in the past shifts.

"Never miss an opportunity to serve" means to always follow your heart's prompting for the kind, the loving, the caring thing to do. Being in service includes anytime you are genuinely caring and considering the welfare and feelings of others. Service is love in action, and it brings you inner peace. This aligns you with your heart and makes you feel not only peaceful but full of energy and vitality. That's because you are creating physical body coherence and full-being coherence: you are aligning to your heart, to who you really are.

Ego's way may still surface, telling you that you need to bypass helping someone to get ahead, or that your good is more important than someone else's. But the more you open to your heart, the more you overcome the limited ego and start living the teaching, "do unto your neighbor as yourself." You then expand your capacity to flow universal love through your own heart. As your heart grows, so does your joy.

Being of service to others means considering others' feelings in any given situation; actively listening to others when they are speaking, be they a co-worker or a child;

letting someone into the intersection; being extra kind at the checkout counter instead of cold and transactional. It means choosing to spend some of your time supporting others, whether that is actual volunteer work, mentoring, or taking time to help a fellow student with their paper or a colleague with their project. It means allowing yourself to be inconvenienced at times to help another.

Being of service also means helping to guide others back to their hearts. By living as a Devoted Heart, you demonstrate what it looks like to be bighearted. This means you can accept others for who they are, and at the same time see them in their highest light. You see them all the way down to the core of the light in their hearts. You can still speak out against what is not right, communicate clearly, and hold a clear line with the values and principles you uphold. And yet you can find a peaceful way through the many, many things you could take issue with, and even retaliate against. This is the way to empower others to open their hearts too.

You start to see that you are okay, much more than okay actually, and so the focus shifts to helping other hearts open. You also share with others the practical ways they can open their hearts too. You see that the more hearts that open, the more society and the world change for the better. Deep in your heart, you know you are part of that change, and so you dedicate your life to supporting heart-opening on the planet in your unique ways as your purpose, or part of your purpose.

Your deepest service requires you to dissolve your ego more and more to transcend into your heart. This requires you to go all the way. All the way to the love inside of you that knows no limits.

Staying Coherent with Compassion

Over time, you can also learn how to keep your heart open, awakened, and in coherence, such as in compassion. Compassion is an energy of high heart intelligence. It means you care, you listen, and you say, "What's the matter? Tell me what's wrong." You can stay in coherence and give love and support, you can be empathetic and still not get dragged down into lower emotions, which creates incoherence and helps no one.

Let's say you learn that your dear friend's mother just received a serious diagnosis. As she weeps on the couch, you weep along with her, melding her pain with your own. The two of you cry for hours, going through a whole box of tissues. At the end, you both feel exhausted and depleted. In contrast, it could look like this: You hold her and listen to her pain, but you hold the space with a coherent heart. You send her love and care, but you remain grounded in your Devoted Heart, and you do not get sucked in. Your strength and balance help to support her back to strength and balance.

Notice how compassion feels rejuvenating and powerful. It stays coherent, and that strength lends itself to actually helping to energize your heart, elevating your own health and well-being, helping to deepen understanding and find intuitive solutions, or simply be deeply present, both for you and for those around you. And ultimately, that's the real way to support others.

GOING ALL THE WAY: RELEASING OLD BLOCKS AND EMBRACING FORGIVENESS

At the Devoted Heart stage, you are in a state of high heart intelligence. You find connection instead of conflict. You grow in feelings of love and care all the time, and it continues to expand. You feel peaceful as a general resting state. And yet, there is still more to go. You can use the power of your coherent heart to keep cleansing out any heart blocks that remain lodged in your subconscious and nervous system. It's as if you fall into a pricker bush and pluck out all the surface thorns, but then you realize, once you got those out of the way, that there are deeper thorns in there still. You could choose to ignore them, and they might hurt, but you could still live. Or, you can decide that you want to go all the way. Getting all the deeper thorns out of our hearts means going all the way to the most powerful love: unconditional love.

The Devoted Heart calls you to go all the way in clearing anything out of your system, out of your field, that is not in alignment with the heart. To do this, you need the deepening of your vision. As your heart's intelligence opens, it paves the path for more clarity, which is also the opening of the inner vision, or the spiritual eye. You're able to see everything more clearly.

You can then see what you're still holding on to. It might be old resentments against others, bigger things that you haven't been able yet to fully forgive, or grievances against yourself that you haven't released. These are all incoherent energies that dim your light and reduce the power of your heart's electromagnetic field. They are like little kinks that need to be worked out to create those huge, powerful waves of energy that bring more success, peace, and happiness to you.

At the earlier heart stages, forgiving and letting go of the deep blame, resentment, and pain—the things you didn't think you could ever get past—would be seen as nothing short of impossible. At this stage, the power of your heart intelligence gives you clear vision: *The only way forward to true freedom is clearing the deepest blockages from your own heart that hinder the full flow of your all-powerful heart intelligence.*

These blocks keep you from feeling the power of your full coherence moving through you, where you fully come on fire: peak performance, magnetism, and feeling the incredible expansion of inner peace and joy in your moment-to-moment experience. These heart blocks are some of the biggest issues that are ultimately keeping you from aligning to your heart, to your True Self.

The more you release troubling thoughts from your subconscious mind, meaning old memories that carry emotional attachment, the more mentally strong you become. A passage in the *Mahabharata* reads, "Forgiveness is quiet of mind." You'll still have the memories, but without the emotional charge that clutters your life by bringing past pain into present events and situations. This frees you to experience real peace and to be the kindhearted person you always wanted to be.

Many of us carry the weight of old resentments. Perhaps it's in what you see as shortcomings in the way your parents and caregivers raised you, or incidents that happened back at school, in your workplace, or with your relatives. No matter what age you were when they occurred, sometimes old grievances feel so heavy you have to release them in pieces.

Forgiveness isn't about endorsing someone's actions or saying what happened is okay. It's not your own judgment about whether someone "deserves" forgiveness or not, if they learned the appropriate lessons or not. Discernment may lead you to choose to distance yourself from someone to protect your well-being, but this choice exists separately from the act of forgiveness.

I'm really thankful that over a decade before she passed, I fully forgave my mom, who loved me immensely, yet was unknowingly verbally critical toward me much of my life. It used to hurt so much, and I used to feel so much anger toward her. As I tapped into my heart more deeply, I could see the situation from her eyes, and that it wasn't so personal. She was just coming from the way that she knew and had learned from my grandmother being critical with her.

It's also essential to forgive *yourself.* If you feel guilty or badly about something hurtful you may have done in the past, the ego can create a mental identification as being "bad" or not worthy of love or good. This dampens the brilliance of your heart. The only way to truly make things better is to learn any lessons, release the guilt, and vow to align to your heart more going forward. In that way, you can shine more brightly for all around you, which is what the world really needs.

At its core, forgiveness is about realigning with your heart center. Whether anger or hurt was "justified" is inconsequential in this context; the emotional and physical toll on you remains consistent, regardless of the cause. If you cling to the belief that your anger is justified, you're really fighting to hold on to a block that limits your heart's true intelligence and brilliant radiance from expanding. Embracing forgiveness is the most energy-efficient path for your spirit. It rejuvenates your health, elevates your well-being, and releases you from the weight of past resentments. Mercy and compassion are the gateways to deeper heart alignment. By crossing this threshold, you'll experience transformative surges in coherence, leading to heightened joy and lightness.

The following practice is a powerful tool to keep releasing stagnation and old heart bondages, and keep going all the way to your heart's intelligence.

HeartAlign
Forgive and Let Go to Freedom Practice

For love to be truly unconditional, the willingness to forgive is necessary. It is the path forward to releasing past resentments, experiences, and judgments that have categorized people as not worthy of love in your mind.

Forgiveness is born of one of the most heart-opening qualities: humility. Humility allows you to let go of the mind's perceptions and surrender to the heart's understanding. You can then recontextualize the experience through the heart's vast intelligence to see where there were limits to understanding and behaviors. And even perhaps where there was innate innocence beneath the ignorance.

Forgiveness is a kind of a miracle. It transforms old, stagnant, and unhealthy energy into the light of higher understanding and vitality. Forgiveness fortifies your life force.

This powerful practice will allow you to utilize your heart's power to dissolve and forgive issues that remain stuck inside of you and are blocking you. The HeartAlign Forgive and Let Go to Freedom Practice is adapted in part from HeartMath's Cut-Thru technique (with permission), which was designed to help people release past hurts and blockages on a cellular level. It was used by participants in the study referred to in the Propelled Heart chapter (Chapter 4), where cortisol went down 23 percent and DHEA increased by 100 percent in one month of practicing this heart coherence technique.

You can practice it when you feel coherent and have more strength to go in and pull out some really deep thorns. For some deeper issues, you may want to do this practice several times to release the issue piece by piece.

1.   Become aware of a resentment or something you
     have not yet forgiven.

2. Relax your body.

3. Shift your awareness into your heart and take some slow, deep breaths.

4. Self-generate the feeling of appreciation by recalling a person or event that allows you to tap into this expansive energy. Then move into the expansiveness of the energy of love and direct it into yourself to heal hurt and pain within you that you still feel from the incidence or person.

5. Dissolve the issue by assuming objectivity, as if you are watching it from a distance.

6. Forgive, piece by piece.

7. Thank your heart for its efforts.

A deeper explanation of each of the steps follows:

1. **Create an awareness of a resentment or something that you have not yet forgiven.** If you can recall something that still bothers you, makes you resentful, and causes you to withhold love in any way, it holds some emotional attachment to the memory and can be addressed now in order to process it, neutralize it, and let it go. Follow your intuition's guidance about which block to focus on at any time.

2. **Relax your body.** You can practice Yogananda's method of tensing and relaxing that is incorporated in the HeartAlign Meditation discussed in the Dark Heart: Incoherence chapter (Chapter 3), or you can simply give your body or your shoulders a little shake to release any pent-up tension. You want to enter this practice with your body as relaxed as possible.

3. **Shift your awareness into your heart and take some slow, deep breaths.** As with the other HeartAlign methods, shift your awareness into your physical and energetic heart area. This heart

awareness helps bring coherence to your heart and brain communication and more coherence to your emotions, which is necessary for this practice to be effective.[67] Take a few slow, deep breaths, pretending that you are breathing in and out of your heart. Start breathing to a count of five breaths in, five breaths out, which translates to six breath cycles per minute—the breath that promotes coherence—then shift into a natural, slow rhythm.

4. **Self-generate the feeling of appreciation. Then move into the expansiveness of the energy of love and direct it into yourself to heal hurt and pain within you that you still feel from the incident or that person.** Your heart's power can heal yourself *first*, and many of us forget this important step. As we heal and discover that we actually *are* okay, and stronger because of anything that may have happened to us, it becomes far easier to forgive others and let go. Self-generate the feeling of appreciation, which means recalling a loved one or past event that evokes this regenerative, coherence-promoting feeling. Then shift into the expansive feeling of love, whether it's with the same loved one or events to help you recall the feeling or a different one. Now direct that energy to the hurt and pain you feel from the incident. It's like metaphysically dressing a wound. Love can heal when directed to do so.

5. **Dissolve the issue by assuming objectivity, as if you are watching it from a distance.** This is where heart intelligence is so powerful. It can help you expand and step back from the situation so you can access deeper understanding. You can then see where someone might have limitations in their understanding or behaviors, where there was misunderstanding, and how you may have played a role as well. This is possible from the heart's power.

If you zoom out and imagine that you are witnessing yourself and the whole scene, or as if it involved other people, you can start to extract yourself from being so overly identified with the issue itself. It's the tight identification, the feeling of violation that the ego holds on to that something happened "to me," that keeps us wrapped into reactions. The more objective you can become, the more you can take the emotional significance out of the event, and the more it can become a memory without great emotions attached to it that bind you to it. Remember this is for your freedom, not the other person's (if there is another involved).

6. **Forgive, piece by piece.** Stay in your heart to try to sincerely dissolve and forgive the issue. This means letting go, and as you do, your heart feels lighter and lighter. Sometimes, one big forgiveness can create an exponential surge of feeling peaceful in your life. This may take place a bit at a time, and you may return here multiple times to fully resolve it. Little by little you can start to forgive and let go, even if it's in little pieces.

7. **Thank your heart for its efforts.** When you feel you have gone as far as you can, come back into appreciating yourself and your own heart for helping you let go of more blocks and for its incredible wisdom and intelligence.

Forgiveness is deep work indeed. But the more you forgive and let go, the more you trade holding on to pain and block-ages in your heart and in your life for lightness, freedom, and the opening of more love to flow through you.

I had a client, whom we will call Mary, who had a deep mother wound. That is, she held great anger and resentment toward her mother for the ways she was treated during her childhood, in which she felt neglected, unseen, and unloved. Even though she had not spoken to her mother in years—who was not invited to her wedding and had not met Mary's two children—her mother somehow made her way semiregularly into conversations. So I knew that there was a heart block that was quite heavy and near the surface just waiting to be processed and healed. Mary had turned to drugs and alcohol for many years and experienced issues like anxiety and chronic acid reflux. Besides some dietary changes that had to be made, it seemed to me that the "acid" of anger was literally spilling out of her!

As with all situations where we have felt great hurt and pain, the journey to forgiveness—a major way to unlock the heart—takes some time. We didn't talk about the situation very much. What we did do was yoga asanas and movement to move energy, and big inhales through the nose and out the mouth. It was the heart that created the healing. She was called to her heart herself, and I supported her own heart healing with meditation and teaching her how to do the HeartAlign Forgive and Let Go to Freedom Practice. As she truly let go, she experienced great peace. This paralleled her career surging into a period of great growth and creativity. She is the most loving mother to her kids. And her acid reflux is also largely healed!

A WARM HEART IS AN ACTIVATED HEART

When someone is warmhearted, it means that those around them are warmed by the all-powerful light of their heart. To be warmhearted is to be deeply nourished by a coherent heart that radiates love and connection. It nourishes you first, and then it nourishes all around you. A warm heart is inclusive. It is attractive. And it is incredibly magnetic. It's like a campfire everyone wants to sit around. You become the light.

Think about that campfire. You have to tend to it. You have to blow into the kindling to warm it up and help it along to grow. You give it attention and add more logs as you need to, to keep feeding the flame. When it's well tended, it provides warmth and energetic nourishment to everyone who sits around it.

So how do you keep your heart warm? You tend to it with your attention and you keep it activated. That means you turn it to the "on" switch by keeping it alive with fresh energy. It stays on no matter what is happening in life around you. You keep it plugged into an inexhaustible source of power: the power of your heart intelligence. Your heart can literally be a warm fire of energy that is always on.

To keep your heart warm and activated in practical terms means that you constantly tune in to its power. It's important to do the practices presented here regularly, as well as any other tools that help you open and awaken your heart intelligence. And beyond that, you transcend into heart-based living. *This means that every action you do and every word you say comes right out of your heart.*

To get there, concentration is a really important tool to cultivate. It overcomes restlessness and distraction. The more you can train yourself to concentrate on your heart, the more you will be receptive to your deeper heart intelligence and the stronger your will to overcome any egoic tendencies that may arise. How do you do that? By regularly practicing the HeartAlign Meditation and other heart-based tools in this book, HeartMath tools, and other highly effective meditation techniques such as Kriya Yoga with increasing focus and concentration. Concentrating within is a skill you must develop, but the rewards are infinite.

As you live and filter all of life through your heart, you begin to notice you are more patient. You feel lighter. You don't get as annoyed when your roommate forgets to unload the dishwasher or the kids are taking forever to get in the car. There's less drama at work and with your friends. Your capacity to remain calm in the midst of chaos grows exponentially during times where you used to become stressed.

There is so much beauty and power that you feel in touch with, right in your heart and right in this moment.

HEART EMBODIMENT:
Lifestyle Tips to Support and Deepen into the Devoted Heart

The following lifestyle practices can further support your deepening into and awakening your Devoted Heart:

- **Practice intuitive cooking and eating.** As the heart opens, along with your intuition, you want to move away from a heady, mental place of eating. There is a much deeper way to nourish yourself, and it requires the intuitive wisdom of being in tune with yourself. Notice if there are certain foods, colors, veggies, fruits, and dishes you are drawn to at any given time. Continue to practice the HeartAlign heart-gut practice discussed in the Propelled Heart chapter (Chapter 4) on a regular basis before making your food choices. You are the best guide for yourself!

- **Eat sweet fruits and berries.** There is a "sweetness" that accompanies the awakening Devoted Heart. The kind of sweet quality that makes one increasingly kind, forgiving, and loving. You can foster more of that energetic sweetness by eating nature's sweet foods, particularly sweet fruits like mangoes, oranges, grapes, and bananas as well as the whole host of berries out there, like blueberries, strawberries, and raspberries. These foods are also super rich in vitality-building antioxidants, minerals, and vitamin C.

- **Bring sacredness and awe to your meals.** To be devoted to the inner world means bringing a sense of sacredness when taking things into your body, including food. It is a powerful, simple daily ritual to take a moment for appreciation, saying grace, or practicing silence while eating your meals. If we don't say grace immediately at family dinnertime, our little one exclaims, "Grace, grace!" Daily rituals remind us that magic—and love—truly are in abundance everywhere.

- **Remove stuck toxins and old waste from your body.** Forgiveness is about letting go of the old, and that is fostered and supported by also keeping your body as cleansed and free of old waste as possible since energy permeates all layers. Spirulina is a powerful green plant to incorporate into your diet. It is grown in water, which is the element that helps to loosen and liberate old matter, and has been shown to chelate, or bind, to heavy metals and other toxins and escort them out of the body. (As someone who has spent many years perpetually constipated to varying degrees, and seeing that many of my clients had the same issues, I have been particularly interested in the healthiest and safest ways to thoroughly cleanse the gastrointestinal tract and body on a regular basis! I created an effective daily cleanse product called Feel Good Detoxy designed to do just that. You can check it out in the Resources section if you are interested.)

Key Points of the Devoted Heart:
Intuition and Forgiveness

- At the Devoted Heart stage, there is such a high level of heart awakening that you become more oriented to the inner world than the outer world.

- Unconditional love and the other heart qualities of love, peace, compassion, appreciation, and care come forward as the dominant energies of your life.

- Because there is much higher heart coherence and greater access to the heart's intelligence at this stage, it becomes easier to create more abundance and success in your creative projects and endeavors.

- Intuition greatly rises, which gives you the ability to access expansive solutions not previously available from the mind alone.

- You now have the strength to let go and forgive resentments and grievances that have blocked you. The powerful HeartAlign Forgive and Let Go to Freedom Practice allows you to do just that.

There's one more heart stage to explore, a stage in which your heart bursts open so much that it unifies and melds with everything inside and outside, and the larger universal heart, so that everything becomes one.

Let's dive in one more time into your beautiful, awakening heart.

Chapter 7

STAGE 5

THE CLEAR HEART: HEART-BRAIN HARMONY

At the Devoted Heart stage, you merged with the coherence and unconditional love inside of your own heart and you now deeply care about all others. At the Clear Heart stage, you go beyond: You merge with the universal heart. Your ego has dissolved completely, and you become one with all hearts everywhere. Spiritually, this is the experience of oneness, or samadhi, as it's known in yoga. It's what Lao-Tzu was referring to when he said, "If you want to know me, look inside your heart."[68]

If you've ever seen a prism, at first it looks quite ordinary because it's simply clear. It's not flashy in any way. But as you hold it up to the sunlight, its true magic is revealed. As the light shines through it, the prism reflects the full spectrum of light as beautiful colors of the rainbow. Like the prism, the Clear Heart is transparent. And in transparency, the light of the larger, universal heart can shine through.

Sri Yukteswar writes, "When all the developments of Ignorance are withdrawn, the heart, being perfectly clear and purified, no longer merely reflects the Spiritual Light but actively manifests the same."[69] Because there is nothing obstructing the heart, it can come into its full, radiant power. The heart simply becomes the light. Light is physical and metaphysical. There is a pattern of light produced by the electromagnetic field of your heart, as we discussed earlier. Your heart literally emits light. And what is the source of the light? In a metaphysical sense, the light is from Source. The greater source of an energetic, brilliant, and higher intelligent power that connects us all.

The Clear Heart is the ultimate stage of the highest heart coherence, where the heart, brain, and mind find clarity and become one. Because of this, the Clear Heart is also the humble heart. It brings you to the realization that no one is better than anyone else. "All souls are equal,"[70] as Yogananda says. *All hearts are fundamentally equal. The Clear Heart is just more transparent.*

We all experience moments of the Clear Heart stage when we move into the ultimate wholeness of now, which is found within us and outside us and everywhere at the same time. It's that expansive, out-of-time-and-space feeling when you stare into your child's eyes, you lose yourself in watching a beautiful sunset, or you sway along at a concert with thousands of others singing to your favorite song.

It is in these moments that you recognize that your heart is already clear, and the deeper you delve into the Clear Heart stage, this realization becomes so strong that it totally silences the ego altogether, so that the mind and the heart become one. This is not out of reach, for it is already in us. We need the clear vision to see it in our own hearts.

THE DEEPEST PEACE

In the fetus, the heart actually forms *before* the brain and starts beating on its own. The brain develops from the bottom up, with the brain stem forming first, then the emotional centers of the amygdala and the hippocampus emerging. The thinking, or rational, brain then grows out of the emotional regions.[71] *In other words, the emotional brain is formed long before the rational brain, and the beating heart is formed before either.* This means that before the thinking brain, we inhabited this space of nonthinking, completely intuitive existence.

The Tao Te Ching says, "Can you cleanse your inner vision, until you see nothing but the light?"[72] It also goes on to say:

Thus the Master is available to all people
and doesn't reject anyone.
He is ready to use all situations
And doesn't waste anything.
This is called embodying the light.[73]

The light sees the light. There's the surface of people, what they look like and what they do and say, but the deeper reality is the light in the heart of all others. Gandhi wrote, "To a pure heart, all hearts are pure."[74] At this stage, you feel whole and see life as whole, because the light is whole.

This means a heart full of peace. The heart becomes crystal clear, free from its own perceptions and judgments that narrow or block the heart in any way. So the heart doesn't "block" life. It is in full peaceful acceptance and harmony with what is.

When you're in the now, there's a deep trust that your destiny works out as it is meant to, and you can rest in that peace. There's a transition from *getting* energy to *receiving* energy. Since you're in alignment with the greater channel of flow, of intelligence, life is allowed to unfold in its own most beautiful, profound, and unobstructed way.

And since you don't put yourself in a box, you don't put others in a box either. You just are, everyone just is, and life just is. The Clear Heart doesn't categorize people as evolved, smart, dumb, or wise. Because of this, everyone feels at home. And peace spreads to other hearts.

A Clear Heart is thoroughly genuine. It's exemplified in a person who is straightforward, with nothing to hide and nothing to defend. The heart and the mind merge into one. When you're in the now, you're the master of your mind and your emotions. When you are nobody from an egoic perspective, you are everybody, for you are the Heart. You are the light that is in all people and all things.

The world also starts to look differently. There is a whole new level of universal harmony that can be perceived beyond what's happening on the surface. Only the clearest of hearts can see the perfection of creation.

Author and psychiatrist David Hawkins describes:

> Everything that exists is perfect and complete. Creation does not move from imperfection to perfection, as is witnessed by the ego, but instead moves from perfection to perfection. The illusion of moving from imperfection to perfection is a mentalization. For example, a rosebud is not an imperfect rose but is a perfect rosebud. When half open, it is a perfect unfolding flower, and when completely opened, it is a perfect open flower. As it fades, it is a perfect faded flower and then becomes a perfect withered plant, which then becomes perfectly dormant.[75]

That vision of eternal perfection means that all of creation is sacred. It is a perspective that is not visible to all heart stages, just like the landscape looks differently from the base, the midway point, and the top of the mountain. And it brings the deepest feelings of peace.

NOBODY AND EVERYBODY

At the Clear Heart stage, the self is the other. The other is you. The experience of oneness, that we are all waves from the same ocean, is not poetry but reality. "Abandoning the vain idea of his separate existence,"[76] as Sri Yukteswar says, we melt into the full aliveness and joy of being whole within ourselves and whole with all of life.

The ego wants to "be someone," to create some kind of name or fame for oneself. It clings to labels, titles, a kind of personality, or what it owns to create a sense of identity for who one is. At this stage all of that vanishes, because we now have the vision to see that trying to categorize the heart reduces its true essence. Energy can't be contained in a little container. The Tao that can be named is not the eternal Tao.

If we follow Ramana Maharshi's meditative question "Who am I? Who am I?" and keep going down to the core, we find that we are beyond any concept that can be named. The Clear Heart dissolves into nothing-ness and emerges as everything-ness. It identifies only with the light within. The heart, the True Self, cannot be named or labeled. It just is.

"The ocean cannot be received in a cup unless the cup is made as large as the ocean,"[77] teaches Paramahansa Yogananda. The "cup" includes all the labels, ideas, and titles; all the ways we identify as professional, mother, uncle, manager, doctor, realtor, assistant, librarian, young, old, smart, not so smart, pretty, plain, better than, less than. It also includes belief systems that close or divide. The ocean is the universal, higher intelligence that can be accessed through the energetic heart. The Clear Heart opens in full transparency to that higher intelligence, and because of that, it radiates with the power of all-ness.

The is-ness of this stage means that in each moment, the heart yields tremendous power, wherever it happens to be. Not power in the sense of pushing its way, but power by fully and totally being in each moment, and so flowing fully with life. No blocks from the past color this moment with emotional memories or skewed reactions. Nothing blocks the power of love. There are no expectations. There's simply showing up in wholeness, with a Clear and transparent heart, and flowing with life in each moment.

This story of Mother Teresa describes the Clear Heart in action:

> After accepting the Nobel Peace Prize, Mother Teresa stopped in Rome on her way back to India from Stockholm. A reporter challenged her about the seeming futility of her efforts. "Mother, you are seventy now," the reporter said. "When you die, the world will be as it was before. What has changed after so much effort?" Mother Teresa responded with a smile. "You know, I never wanted to change the world. I have only tried to be a drop of pure water in which God's love can be reflected. Does that seem like a small thing to you?"[78]

There's an untouchable joy at this stage. And that's because, as Sri Yukteswar teaches, the Clear Heart has realized "the nothingness of the external world" and instead becomes the "Omnipotent Love in the core of the heart."[79] The *Bhagavad Gita* lists one of the soul qualities, "radiance of character," which is described as someone with spiritual magnetism, with "a quiet outer expression of deep inner joy."[80] Radiance is the word that seems to best describe the radiant energy and brilliant light emitting from someone who is at this level of full heart awakening.

Living in full transparency with life means there is bliss and joy to be found anywhere and everywhere. The Clear Heart is ever-present, aware, and open to life in each moment, whether you're feeding the dog, staring out the window, or walking around the grocery store. Joy is found when you put your heart into each moment.

MIRACLES ARISE

With its transparency, the Clear Heart merges seamlessly with everything, forging a deep interconnectedness that paves the way for synchronicities. This alignment facilitates events that appear nothing short of miraculous—occurrences that a linear mind might never deem possible.

Yogananda teaches us, "But as soon as you meditate and permit your consciousness to retire within to its source, the immortal soul, you realize that you are not subject to these limiting patterns."[81] Miracles are of the higher intelligence, which moves in ways that are nonlinear and not comprehensible to the intellectual mind alone. The truly wonderous manifests through perfect harmony with one's heart field and the greater field.

These miracles are not the result of a particular person. They are impersonal and are because of the power of the energy field moving *through* them. The classic Western hero stories usually culminate in the protagonist overcoming their self-doubt and believing "I have the power." The Clear Heart realizes the truth instead, that "A greater power is moving through me." Gandhi said, "There is a force in the universe, which, if we permit it, will flow through us and produce miraculous results."[82]

In the Indian epic the *Ramayana*, Hanuman, a Hindu deity, is brought before the court as a hero for rescuing Sita, wife of the deity Rama, from the palace of the demon Ravana. He dismisses the emerald ring given for his reward, which bewilders the crowd. Instead, he opens up his chest to reveal the deities of Sita and Rama depicted in the middle of his heart, acknowledging that there is something much more powerful within him that he is both merged with and in service to. That something needs no reward or recognition.

There is still some thinking, of course, in a practical sense, but all extraneous thinking and evaluating have dissolved. This is what Lao-Tzu is referring to when he says, "He doesn't think about his actions; they flow from the core of his being."[83] Gone are the questions, *Am I doing this right? Should I do this or that?* Your actions become one with your heart. The division between you and others dissolves. The separation between questions and answers dissolves. There is just life, just being. One simply becomes an instrument as part of the larger unfolding of life. The mind is silent.

One of the ways you move beyond thinking is to be totally clear inside. That is, to have a clear conscience. The more you do the right thing, not just for yourself but for the good of others—the more you clean up any past situations, and digest and process any old memories stuck within you—the more clear your conscience will become.

Yogananda says, "When your conscience is clear, when you know you are doing right, you are not afraid of anything."[84] A fearless heart can then fully open and hold the space for miracles and amazing synchronicities.

Self-Transcendence

In his later years, psychologist Abraham Maslow revised his pyramid of the hierarchy of needs to add another stage beyond self-actualization. He called it *self-transcendence*. Maslow says that, "Transcendence refers to the very highest and most inclusive or holistic levels of human consciousness, behaving and relating, as ends rather than means, to oneself, to significant others, to human beings in general, to other species, to nature, and to the cosmos."[85] Maslow proposed that one of the main characteristic of self-transcended people is autonomy and independence from culture and environment[86]. They do not need the approval of others, and their opinions are not formed from the immediate circumstances in which they find themselves. Self-transcendence is reached when a person seeks to further a cause beyond the self and identifies with something greater than the individual self.[87]

At this level of transcendence, some speak very little. The great yoga guru Lahiri Mahasaya spoke little, though he attracted droves of people from all around India to be in his presence. Saint Francis of Assisi increasingly turned to a life of solitude and prayer for the poor in isolation, eventually becoming a hermit. The great yogi Mahavatar Babaji remained a recluse in a Himalayan cave.

Transcendence is born of transparency. We transcend ourselves when we let go of ourselves and connect to something far greater. Metaphorically, we throw ourselves into the flame of the heart's eternal love and burn away all that is not of love, all that is not of the heart. Then only the heart is left and only that which connects us deeply to ourselves and all others and all of life.

THE POWER OF YOUR CONNECTION

Your heart's coherent and luminous field aids in healing the world and those around you. In reality, these individual fields merge into a singular, elevated field. At this level, we realize the truth of the principle of nondualism—the inherent oneness of all. We're more than just interconnected; we're unified by a singular, vast intelligence. We're all part of the same vast ocean, each wave undeniably connected to the whole.

Higher coherence can overcome chaos, which is why your heart's intelligence gives you the power to overcome negative thoughts and limited patterns. It can also heal other's hearts. A coherent heart is of great power in the world. Research from the HeartMath Institute found that when people touch, such as holding hands or simply standing closely together, the electrical energy from one heart is transmitted to the other person's brain waves and vice versa.[88] What this means is that your energy—your electromagnetic energy—affects and influences those around you. You can also be affected by others, as mentioned in the Dark Heart chapter (Chapter 3), but since you are in a powerful state of coherence in the Clear Heart, your heart becomes a light in the dark.

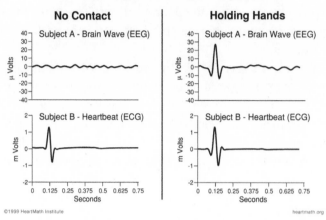

Heartbeat signal-averaged waveforms showing a transference of the electrical energy generated by Subject B's heart can be detected in Subject A's EEG (brain waves) when they hold hands. (Courtesy of the HeartMath Institute, 2024.)

If you're flowing in an emotion like care while you touch others, you can promote health and well-being in others.[89] We know that a caring touch from a nurse or doctor can make all the difference. We intuitively feel how a hug from a loved one is healing. There is much clinical research to back up what you instinctively know about caring touch, including that it has helped asthmatic children improve breathing function and sleepless babies fall asleep;[90] it has also been shown to increase adults' well-being and health.[91]

In the most advanced stage of heart development, you'll recognize that your heart is an endless wellspring of love, peace, and joy. Life then revolves around embodying this energy and sharing it with others. Even when compared to the highly compassionate stage of the Devoted Heart, the Clear Heart further commits itself to service. Life's primary purpose becomes centered around service—your main objective becomes sharing this love and care with those around you.

You are in service just by emitting a coherent heart energy field of light that everyone around you can feel. And you are also in service by radiating unconditional love, kindness, and goodwill to all who come in contact with you.

An intentional way to be in service is in completing the following practice, which teaches you how to consciously broadcast your own heart's energy out into the world.

HeartAlign Heart Broadcast Practice

This practice is about using the power and intelligence of love in a practical way. You can always be of service and be a healing force on the planet by intentionally broadcasting love out into the greater field of the world. All energy fields interconnect.

At the same time, this practice creates a high level of coherence in yourself by saturating you with the highest intelligence that exists—love. So as you intend to serve others in this way, your own health and vitality will also build. The more you give, the more you also receive.

- Shift your attention to your heart.

- Breathe in love, and as you exhale, send that love to all the cells and organs of your body and all parts of your being.

- Breathe in love, and as you exhale, broadcast the energy of love out of your heart and into the world.

Greater explanation of these steps follows.

- **Shift your attention to your heart.** It always begins right here! Place your full attention right on your heart, forgetting everything else.

- **Breathe in love, and as you exhale, send that love to all the cells and organs of your body and all parts of your being.** Tap into the all-powerful energy of love that is always there to be accessed. You can go right to the feeling, or similarly to how you self-generated appreciation in other HeartAlign practices, you can self-generate love by recalling a loved one, a situation, or an event that helps you drop into that all-expansive energy. Sustain the feeling of love within you, breathing it in and with every exhale, sending it to every cell in your body and all parts of your entire being, until you saturate yourself in love.

- **Breathe in love, and as you exhale, broadcast the energy of love out of your heart and into the world.** Notice how the most gentle, yet fullest of breaths allows you to feel the power of love. Love is of the highest intelligence and never needs to force. As you exhale, send out the love to those in your immediate surroundings and then out in the greater world, especially to areas that need extra healing and peace. Know—and feel—that your heart's electromagnetic field is part of the greater field connecting all things and all people. And that your light and love can amplify the light and the love of the world.

Global Coherence Initiative

Global coherence refers to the synchronized and harmonious order not only within the individual body's systems but also in a group or in the collective. A growing body of evidence suggests that there is an energetic field that connects the entire collective. The scientific community is just beginning to appreciate and understand the deeper level of how we are interconnected. Sociologist Raymond Bradley, in collaboration with eminent brain researcher, neuroscientist, and neurosurgeon Karl Pribram, found that most groups have some kind of emotional energetic connection between virtually all members.[92]

Research on global coherence encompasses a large variety of scientific data to gain new insights into the interconnectedness of human behavior, human health, the sun and earth's magnetic activity, social unrest and significant global events, and more, which scientists have discussed for decades. See the Resources section if you are interested in learning more about HeartMath Institute's Global Coherence Initiative (GCI).

AFFIRMATION MANTRA

You can repeat the following mantra as an affirmation to keep connecting you to the truth in your heart. In Yogananda's method of practicing mantras, you repeat the affirmation mantra out loud in a normal speaking voice, then start to whisper it, and then finally say it silently within yourself, merging with the energy behind the words.

Practice this mantra after you do the HeartAlign Meditation, keeping your full concentration on your heart, and anytime you feel called to really connect to your heart during the day.

I am the heart.

I am the light.

I am the unlimited love of the True Self within the heart.

My heart is a light that shows other hearts the truth of their light too.

I am the heart.

HEART EMBODIMENT:
Lifestyle Tips to Support the Awakening of the Clear Heart

The following lifestyle practices can further support your deepening into and awakening of your Clear Heart:

- **Embrace simplicity.** We realize, at some point, that we simply don't need excess clutter. More is not more. Simple is more, because the simple way is the clear way forward. Try simplifying your lifestyle, your needs, your surroundings, your daily schedule, and your meals. For example, your food can still be delicious, but it can be more simply prepared, with a bigger focus on the freshness of the ingredients. Ask your heart how this is possible to do across your life.

- **Eat more raw food and sprouts.** Raw foods are truly powerful because they contain the unadulterated, unaltered nutrition born of nature. Try eating more raw veggies and fruit. You may have to build up your digestive power over time, along with your digestive enzymes, which help you effectively break down food and are very helpful to take. Also incorporate sprouts, which you can add to any dish or salad. Sprouts are full of life force and contain large amounts of easily assimilated and digestible nutrients like proteins, fatty acids, minerals, and vitamins. They are one of the most effective foods to help increase your vitality, which further supports the most profound energetic heart unlocking.

- **Ground in nature.** The energy of feeling oneness, where the separation or perceived gaps between you and anything else disappears, fosters great abundance. This oneness, experienced at this stage as the complete harmony between your heart and your head, is the Clear Heart. And you can also promote experiencing oneness energy by grounding in nature and making direct contact with the earth as much as possible. Take off your shoes and walk at a beach or at a park barefoot, try hiking barefoot through the trails and mud (like my family loves to do!), or lay fully on your back on the lawn and look up at the starry sky. The more you can deeply connect to nature, the more you can connect to your own heart!

Key Points of the Clear Heart: Heart-Brain Harmony

- The Clear Heart is the highest human heart stage, where one's heart becomes transparent and melds with the universal heart.

- At this stage, one experiences unity, deep connection, and unshakeable inner peace.

- This stage corresponds to the highest level of heart coherence, known as heart-brain harmony, where the heart, brain, and mind find ultimate clarity and become one.

- The highest heart qualities flow through you fully and constantly, including compassion, peace, appreciation, bliss, and love.

- The HeartAlign Heart Broadcast Practice allows you to intentionally be of service and a healing force on the planet by sending out love into the world

- This stage enables the highest levels of intuitive knowing as well as great synchronicities and the seeming miraculous.

As we wrap up our journey to the heart together, I hope you feel inspired to keep awakening your amazing heart. Our journey to the heart is ongoing. I encourage you to reread this book as you feel called to, for your heart is dynamic and will increasingly become open and receptive to more information and in different ways.

Please continue to practice, with sincerity and concentration, the tools and practices offered here as well, and your heart's magnificent intelligence and coherence will continue to grow for the rest of your days to ever-expanding levels.

It is exciting to know that all you need and want is inside of your heart, and it's here right now. You just have to let your heart guide your way back to realizing who you really are.

CONCLUSION: THE HEART-FORWARD PATH

Mother Teresa said:

"If we were more willing to see the good and the beautiful things that surround us, we would be able to transform our families. From there, we would change our next-door neighbors and then others who live in our neighborhood or city. We would be able to bring peace and love to our world, which hungers so much for these things."[93]

We are all able to bring great change into our lives and into the world from our hearts. The heart can see the good and the beautiful that is sometimes below the surface. The heart holds the expansive heart intelligence to overcome division and see through to harmony and love.

The following is an excerpt from The Cosmic Sphere of Love[94], a meditation exercise by Paramahansa Yogananda:

Concentrate on a sphere of love within your heart, filled with light that is ever-expanding, encompassing your body, everyone around you, all nations, the whole earth, in a nimbus of glory.

Now that great sphere of love holds within its bosom all planets, the Milky Way, all island universes, and every one of us. In that cosmic love see the harmony restored in all parts of the earth and the universe[95].

Your heart holds the key to your greatest power: your power to bring love and compassion and care into the world. Your heart can transform you on all levels—physically, emotionally, mentally, and spiritually—and then it can radiate out and transform the world around you and beyond.

The intention of this book is to help you awaken to your own true power. Please use it. The world needs your awakened heart.

RESOURCES

Solluna is a holistic lifestyle brand that I founded to support you on your journey to connecting to the wholeness in your heart and your True Self! It contains offerings across our Four Cornerstone philosophy: food, body, emotional well-being and spiritual growth. Please visit **www. MySolluna.com**, our central hub for:

- Complimentary HeartAlign Meditation tracks

- Solluna SBO Probiotics, the Feel Good Detoxy daily cleanse product, and other digestive products

- The Glowing Greens Powder

- Hundreds of recipes, such as the Glowing Greens Powder Smoothie, the Power Protein Smoothie, and elixirs

- The *Feel Good Podcast* with Kimberly Snyder

- And much more!

RECOMMENDED BOOKS AND PROGRAMS

- *Autobiography of a Yogi,* by Paramahansa Yogananda

- *The Holy Science,* by Swami Sri Yukteswar

- *The Self-Realization Fellowship Lessons* (to learn Kriya yoga), available at yogananda.org/lessons

- *To Be Victorious in Life,* by Paramahansa Yogananda

- *Man's Eternal Quest,* by Paramahansa Yogananda

- *You Are More Than You Think You Are,* by Kimberly Snyder

- *The Beauty Detox Solution,* by Kimberly Snyder

- *Heart Intelligence,* by Doc Childre, Howard Martin, Dr. Deborah Rozman and Dr. Rollin McCraty

- *The HeartMath Solution*, by Doc Childre and Howard Martin

- The HeartMath App (to track and increase your heart coherence), available in the Apple app store and Google Play store

- The HeartMath Inner Balance Coherence Plus sensor (to track and increase your HRV coherence for high performance), available at HeartMath.com

- The Global Coherence Initiative, by HeartMath Institute, a science-based project to unite people in heart-focused love and intention, to facilitate the shift in global consciousness, available at Heartmath.org/gci

ENDNOTES

1. Rollin McCraty, *Science of the Heart: Exploring the Role of the Heart in Human Performance*, vol. 2 (Boulder Creek, CA: HeartMath Institute, 2015), 1–2, 8, 26, 53–65.

2. McCraty, *Science of the Heart*, 5.

3. Doc Childre et al., *Heart Intelligence: Connecting with the Heart's Intuitive Guidance for Effective Choices and Solutions* (Dundee, Scotland: Waterfront Digital Press, 2016), 29.

4. Sri Yukteswar originally referred to the fifth heart stage as the *Clean Heart*. In my modern interpretation, I decided to shift this stage to the *Clear Heart* because I believe this phrase best conveys in a modern context the essence of this heart stage.

5. Paramahansa Yogananda, *Spiritual Diary: An Inspirational Thought for Each Day of the Year,* 2nd ed. (Los Angeles: Self-Realization Fellowship, 2005), September 24.

6. Swami Sri Yukteswar, *The Holy Science.* eighth edition. (Los Angeles: Self-Realization Fellowship, 1990), 77.

7. Paramahansa Yogananda, *Journey to Self-Realization* (Los Angeles: Self-Realization Fellowship, 1997), 410.

8. Yogananda, *Journey to Self-Realization.*

9. Rollin McCraty, Deborah Rosman, and Doc Childre, eds., *HeartMath: A New Biobehavioral Intervention for Increasing Health and Personal Effectiveness—Increasing Coherence in the Human System* (Amsterdam: Harwood Academic Publishers, 1999); L. Z. Song, G. E. Schwartz, and L. G. Russek, "Heart-Focused Attention and Heart-Brain Synchronization: Energetic and Physiological Mechanisms," *Alternative Therapies in Health and Medicine* 4, no. 5 (September 1998): 44–62; and Rollin McCraty, William A. Tiller, and Mike Atkinson, "Head-Heart Entrainment: A Preliminary Survey," in *Proceedings of the Brain-Mind Applied Neurophysiology EEG Neurofeedback Meeting*, Key West, FL, February 1996.

10. Rollin McCraty et al., "The Effects of Emotions on Short-Term Power Spectrum Analysis of Heart Rate Variability," *American Journal of Cardiology* 76, no. 14 (Nov. 15, 1995): 1083–93; McCraty, Tiller, and Atkinson, "Head-Heart Entrainment"; Rollin McCraty, Mike Atkinson, and William A. Tiller, "New Electrophysiological Correlates Associated with Intentional Heart Focus," *Subtle Energies* 4, no. 3 (1993): 251–68; and William Tiller, Rollin McCraty, and Mike Atkinson, "Cardiac Coherence: A New Non-invasive Measure of Autonomic System Order," *Alternative Therapies in Health and Medicine* 2, no. 1 1996): 52–65.

11. Joseph LeDoux, *The Emotional Brain: The Mysterious Underpinnings of Emotional Life* (New York: Simon & Schuster, 1996).

12. Glen Rein, Mike Atkinson, and Rollin McCraty, "The Physiological and Psychological Effects of Compassion and Anger," *Journal of Advancement in Medicine* 8, no. 2 (Summer 1995): 87–105.

13. Yukteswar, *The Holy Science*, 45.

14. Robert C. Frysinger and Ronald M. Harper, "Cardiac and Respiratory Correlations with Unit Discharge in Epileptic Human Temporal Lobe," *Epilepsia* 31, no. 2 (April 1990): 162–71. https://onlinelibrary.wiley.com/doi/abs/10.1111/j.1528-1167.1990.tb06301.x

15. Kimberly Snyder et al., *The HeartAlign Meditation Study* (Los Angeles: HeartMath Institute, 2023).

16. Snyder et al., *HeartAlign Meditation Study*,

17. McCraty et al., "The Effects of Emotions"; McCraty, Tiller, and Atkinson, "Head-Heart Entrainment"; McCraty, Atkinson, and Tiller, "New Electrophysiological Correlates," 251–68; and Tiller, McCraty, and Atkinson, "Cardiac Coherence," 52–65.

18. Rollin McCraty et al., "The Coherent Heart: Heart-Brain Interactions, Psychophysiological Coherence, and the Emergence of System-Wide Order," *Integral Review* 5, no. 2 (December 2009): 101–15; and Abdullah A. Alabdulgader, "Coherence: A Novel Nonpharmacological Modality for Lowering Blood Pressure in Hypertensive Patients," *Global Advances in Health and Medicine* 1, no. 2 (May 2012): 56-64.

19. Doc Childre and Howard Martin, *The HeartMath Solution* (New York: HarperCollins, 1999), 105.

20. McCraty, Tiller, and Atkinson, "Head-Heart Entrainment."

21. McCraty et al., "The Effects of Emotions."

22. Tiller, McCraty, and Atkinson, "Cardiac Coherence," 52–65."

23. Rollin McCraty et al., "Music Enhances the Effect of Positive Emotional States on Salivary IgA," *Stress Medicine* 12, no. 3 (July 1996): 167–75.

24. Rein, Atkinson, and McCraty, "The Physiological and Psychological Effects of Compassion and Anger."

25. Song, Schwartz, and Russek, "Heart-Focused Attention and Heart-Brain Synchronization," 44–62.

26. McCraty, Rosman, and Childre, *HeartMath: A New Biobehavioral Intervention*; and Rollin McCraty et al., "The Electricity of Touch: Detection and Measurement of Cardiac Energy Exchange between People," in *Brain and Values: Is a Biological Science of Values Possible*, ed. Karl H. Pribram (Mahwah, NJ: Lawrence Erlbaum Associates, 1998), 359–79.

27. Paramahansa Yogananda, *Man's Eternal Quest: Collected Talks & Essays on Realizing God in Daily Life* (Los Angeles: Self-Realization Fellowship, 1982), 79.

28. Yukteswar, *The Holy Science*, 78–79.

29. Sandra Blakeslee, "Complex and Hidden Brain in the Gut Makes Stomachaches and Butterflies," *New York Times*, Jan. 23, 1996, Section C, C1.

30. Blakeslee, "Complex and Hidden Brain," *New York Times*.

31. McCraty, Tiller, and Atkinson, "Head-Heart Entrainment."

32. McCraty et al., "The Effects of Emotions,"; and Childre and Martin, *The HeartMath Solution*, 38.

33. Yogananda, *Journey to Self-Realization*, 89–90.

34. D. S. Kerr et al., "Chronic Stress-Induced Acceleration of Electrophysiologic and Morphometric Biomarkers of Hippocampal Aging," *Journal of Neuroscience* 11, no. 5 (May 1991): 1316–17; and Robert M. Sapolsky, *Stress, the Aging Brain, and the Mechanisms of Neuron Death* (Cambridge, MA: MIT Press, 1992).

35. Robert M. Berne and Mathew N. Levy, *Physiology*, 3rd ed. (St. Louis: Mosby, 1993).

36. S. C. Manolagas, D. C. Anderson, and R. Lindsay, "Adrenal Steroids and the Development of Osteoporosis in the Oophorectomized Women," *Lancet* 2 (September 22, 1979), 597.

37. P. De Feo et al., "Contribution of Cortisol to Glucose Counterregulation in Humans," *American Journal of Physiology* 257, no. 1 (July 1989): E35-E42.

38. Per Mårin et al., "Cortisol Secretion in Relation to Body Fat Distribution in Obese Premenopausal Women," *Metabolism* 41, no. 8 (August 1992): 882–86.

39. McCraty et al., "The Impact of a New Emotional Self-Management Program," 151–70.

40. Yogananda, *Journey to Self-Realization,* 104.

41. McCraty et al., "The Effects of Emotions"; McCraty, Tiller, and Atkinson, "Head-Heart Entrainment"; McCraty, Atkinson, and Tiller, "New Electrophysiological Correlates," 251–68; and Tiller, McCraty, and Atkinson, "Cardiac Coherence," 52–65.

42. R. K. Prabhu and U. R. Rao, *Mind of Mahatma Gandhi* (Ahemadabad, India: Navajivan Mudranalaya, 1968).

43. Vincent Sheean, *Lead, Kindly Light: Gandhi and the Way to Peace* (n.p.: Borodino Books, 2018).

44. Ibid. Sheean, *Lead, Kindly Light.*

45. Hitendra Wadhwa, *Inner Mastery, Outer Impact: How Your Five Core Energies Hold the Key to Success,* (New York: Hachette Books, 2022), 289.

46. Yukteswar, *The Holy Science,* 51.

47. Ralph Waldo Emerson, *Self-Reliance* (White Plains, NY: Peter Pauper Press, 1967).

48. LeDoux, *The Emotional Brain.*

49. Aron Siegman et al., "Dimensions of Anger and CHD in Men and Women: Self-Ratings versus Spouse Ratings," *Journal of Behavioral Medicine* 21, no. 4 (August 1998): 315–36.

50. McCraty, *Science of the Heart,* 11.

51. McCraty, *Science of the Heart,* 26-27.

52. Laura Pringle, e-mail message to author, November 29th, 2023.

53. Yogananda, *Journey to Self-Realization,* 272.

54. Yukteswar, *The Holy Science,* 55.

55. Yukteswar, *The Holy Science,* 95.

56. Brother Premamoy, *Bringing Out the Best in Our Relationships With Others* (Los Angeles: Self-Realization Fellowship, 1983), 25.

57. Yogananda, *Man's Eternal Quest,* 73.

58. Yukteswar, *The Holy Science,* 82.

59. J. Armour, "Neurocardiology: Anatomical and Functional Principles," in McCraty, Rosman, and Childre, *HeartMath: A New Biobehavioral Intervention;* John I. Lacey and Beatrice C. Lacey, "Some Autonomic-Central Nervous System Interrelationships," in *Physiological Correlates of Emotion,* ed. Perry Black (New York: Academic Press, 1970), 205–27; J. Koriath and E. Lindholm, "Cardiac-Related Cortical Inhibition During a Fixed Foreperiod Reaction Time Task," *International Journal of Psychophysiology* 4, no. 3 (November 1986): 183–95; and Rainier Schandry and Pedro Montoya, "Event-

Related Brain Potentials and the Processing of Cardiac Activity,"
Biological Psychology 42, no. 1–2 (January 5, 1996): 75–85.

60. McCraty, Tiller, and Atkinson, "Head-Heart Entrainment."

61. Yogananda, *Journey to Self-Realization*, 309.

62. Yogananda, *Journey to Self-Realization*, 308.

63. Albert Einstein, *The Albert Einstein Collection: Essays in Humanism, The Theory of Relativity, and The World As I See It*," (New York: Open Road Media, 2016), 182.

64. Paramahansa Yogananda, "How to Succeed in Finding God," *Self-Realization Magazine*, (Summer 2008), 10.

65. The Harvard newspaper reported: "Mother Teresa Speaks Her Mind," *Harvard Magazine*, April 25, 2011, www.harvardmagazine.com/2011/04/greatest-hits-mother-teresa.

66. Yogananda, *Journey to Self-Realization*, 276.

67. McCraty et al., "The Effects of Emotions"; McCraty, Tiller, and Atkinson, "Head-Heart Entrainment"; McCraty, Atkinson, and Tiller, "New Electrophysiological Correlates," 251–68; and Tiller, McCraty, and Atkinson, "Cardiac Coherence," 52–65.

68. Lao-Tzu, *Tao Te Ching*, trans. Stephen Mitchell (New York: HarperCollins, 1988), verse 70.

69. Yukteswar, *The Holy Science*, 41.

70. *Sayings of Paramahansa Yogananda* (Los Angeles: The Self Realization Fellowship, 1980), 21.

71. Childre and Martin, *The HeartMath Solution*, 9.

72. Lao-Tzu, *Tao Te Ching*, verse 10.

73. Lao-Tzu, *Tao Te Ching*, verse 27.

74. *Gandhi Literature: Collected Works of Mahatma Gandhi*. Volumes 1 to 98. http://www.gandhiashramsevagram.org/gandhi-literature/collected-works-of-mahatma-gandhi-volume-1-to-98.php.

75. David R. Hawkins, *Transcending the Levels of Consciousness: The Stairway to Enlightenment* (United States: Hay House, 2006), 280.

76. Yukteswar, *The Holy Science*, 53.

77. Yogananda, *Journey to Self-Realization*, 221.

78. Leo Maasburg, *Mother Teresa of Calcutta. A Personal Portrait: 50 Inspiring Stories Never Before Told* (Ignatius Press: 2015), 194.

79. Yukteswar, *The Holy Science*, 39, 36.

80. Paramahansa Yogananda, *God Talks with Arjuna: The Bhagavad Gita: Royal Science of God-Realization,* 2 vols. (Los Angeles: Self-Realization Fellowship, 1995), 966.

81. Yogananda, *Journey to Self-Realization,* 405.

82. Peta Morton. *Ancient Teachings for Modern Times* (Hunt, John Publishing, 2019).

83. Lao-Tzu, *Tao Te Ching,* verse 50.

84. Yogananda, *Journey to Self-Realization,* 274.

85. Maslow, A. H. (1971). *The Farther Reaches of Human Nature.* (New York, Arkana/Penguin Books), 269.

86. Maslow, A.H. (1973). Self-actualizing people: A study of psychological health. In R.J.

87. Lowry (Ed.), Dominance, Self-Eteem, Self-Actualization: Germinal papers of A.H. Maslow (Monterey, CA: Brooks/Cole), 177-200.

88. Koltko-Rivera, M.E. (2006). Rediscovering the later version of Maslow's hierarchy of needs: Selftranscendence and opportunities for theory, research, and unification.

89. *Review of General Psychology,* 10(4), 302-317.

90. McCraty et al., "The Electricity of Touch," 359–79 and McCraty, Rosman, and Childre, *HeartMath: A New Biobehavioral Intervention.*

91. McCraty et al., "The Electricity of Touch," 359–79.

92. Tiffany Field, "Massage Therapy for Infants and Children," *Journal of Developmental & Behavioral Pediatrics* 16, no. 2 (April 1995): 105–11.

93. Gail Ironson et al., "Massage Therapy Is Associated with Enhancement of the Immune System's Cytotoxic Capacity," *International Journal of Neuroscience* 84, no. 1–4 (1996): 205–17.

94. Raymond Trevor Bradley, *Charisma and Social Structure: A Study of Love and Power, Wholeness and Transformation* (New York: Paragon House, 1987.

95. Mother Teresa. *No Greater Love (*New World Library, 2016).

96. Paramhansa Ygananda, "The Cosmic Sphere of Love." *Self-Realization* Magazine (Annual Issue, 2022), 57.

97. Ibid.

ACKNOWLEDGMENTS

I am so incredibly grateful and appreciative to the many people who have supported the creation of this book. First of all, I want to thank Hay House, from the bottom of my heart, for believing in this book's message and being my partner in bringing it forward into the world. Thank you to Reid Tracy, Patty Gift, and Allison Janice, as well as my wonderful editor Melody Guy. And thank you to Lara Asher, for also helping with the edits! With great love, I would also love to thank the writer Gary Jansen, for being my longtime dear friend, always there to encourage me to clarify my ideas, who was with me every step of the way with this book. Thank you, Gary, with my whole heart.

There are no words for the deepest of gratitude I have for Paramahansa Yogananda, Swami Sri Yukteswar, and the whole line of Self-Realization Fellowship gurus, for their indelible impact across the whole of my life and the life-changing knowledge and wisdom that they brought to this earth. This soul humbly thanks you with my whole heart, forever and ever.

I have deep love and appreciation for the HeartMath Institute, especially Doc Childre, Deborah Rozman, Rollin McCraty, and Howard Martin. Thank you for your great support, for sharing your amazing research and work on heart intelligence and heart awakening with me and the world, and for conducting the HeartAlign Meditation Study with me.

I couldn't carry out my work and writing without the support of my dearest friend and longtime partner, John Pisani, godson to my children and a vitally important part of my family and life. Thank you for everything, and for your huge heart. I am also so grateful for Katelyn Hughes, always loving and kind. She's a creative powerhouse who has been a vital part of supporting my work for over a decade, and also Solluna. I love and appreciate you so much! I am also incredibly grateful for the rest of my amazing Solluna team. And I have the deepest appreciation for Laura Pringle. You are truly a blessing, and I am so grateful for you and all your support! I am so grateful to Faith and Justice Collier, for the unwavering support during the writing of this book, including generously gifting me my one of a kind Indian writing desk for my writing cabin. Thank you Faith, for our many inspiring, heart-heart conversations! Thank you to Elena Reyes, for your beautiful heart and all your invaluable support in my home during the writing of this book. And thank you to all the other friends and the amazing support system I am so blessed to have! Thank you to my amazing parents, Bruce and Sally, for being a part of my soul family. I bow down in gratitude for our enormous love and all the growth we have been through together. Our love is everlasting.

Thank you to my beloved sons, Emerson and Moses. Thank you for choosing me to be your Mama. As we say, "I love you to the moon and back a million times . . . and infinitely more than that." Thank you for all that you have taught me about love, and most of all, for simply being the beautiful souls that you are. I love you forever, and you are held in my heart for eternity.

Last but certainly not least, I want to thank my soulmate, my mirror, one of the greatest blessings of my life, my husband, Jon. I am grateful for you and more in love with you each day. Our love is a miracle.

ABOUT THE AUTHOR

Kimberly Snyder is a *New York Times* best-selling author, spiritual and meditation teacher, international speaker, nutritionist, and holistic wellness expert. She has authored seven books, including *Radical Beauty*, which she co-authored with Deepak Chopra, and *You Are More Than You Think You Are: Practical Enlightenment for Everyday Life.*

She is also the founder of Solluna, a holistic lifestyle brand that offers supplements, meditations, and courses, as well as the HeartAlign System and Meditation. Kimberly is the host of the top-rated *Feel Good Podcast*, which covers all aspects of holistic wellness.

Kimberly has worked with dozens of top celebrities to feel their best, including Drew Barrymore, Reese Witherspoon, and Channing Tatum, and is regularly featured on numerous national media outlets, including *Good Morning America,* the *Today* show, *The New York Times, Vogue,* and *The Wall Street Journal.* Kimberly resides in Los Angeles and Hawai'i with her husband and children. To learn more about Kimberly and Solluna, visit: **www.mysolluna.com** and **@_kimberlysnyder.**

Hay House Titles of Related Interest

YOU CAN HEAL YOUR LIFE, the movie,
starring Louise Hay & Friends
(available as an online streaming video)
www.hayhouse.com/louise-movie

THE SHIFT, the movie,
starring Dr. Wayne W. Dyer
(available as an online streaming video)
www.hayhouse.com/the-shift-movie

***

THE HIGH FIVE HABIT: Take Control of Your Life with One Simple Habit, by Mel Robbins

LIVING THE WISDOM OF THE TAO: The Complete Tao Te Ching and Affirmations, by Wayne Dyer

POWER VS. FORCE: The Hidden Determinants of Human Behavior, by Dr. David R. Hawkins

YOGA, POWER & SPIRIT: Patanjali the Shaman, by Alberto Villoldo, Ph.D.

YOU ARE MORE THAN YOU THINK YOU ARE: Practical Enlightenment for Everyday Life, by Kimberly Snyder

All of the above are available at your local bookstore,
or may be ordered by contacting Hay House (see next page).

We hope you enjoyed this Hay House book. If you'd like to receive our online catalog featuring additional information on Hay House books and products, or if you'd like to find out more about the Hay Foundation, please contact:

Hay House LLC, P.O. Box 5100, Carlsbad, CA 92018-5100
(760) 431-7695 or (800) 654-5126
www.hayhouse.com® • www.hayfoundation.org

———

Published in Australia by:
Hay House Australia Publishing Pty Ltd
18/36 Ralph St., Alexandria NSW 2015
Phone: +61 (02) 9669 4299
www.hayhouse.com.au

Published in the United Kingdom by:
Hay House UK Ltd
The Sixth Floor, Watson House,
54 Baker Street, London W1U 7BU
Phone: +44 (0) 203 927 7290
www.hayhouse.co.uk

Published in India by:
Hay House Publishers (India) Pvt Ltd
Muskaan Complex, Plot No. 3,
B-2, Vasant Kunj, New Delhi 110 070
Phone: +91 11 41761620
www.hayhouse.co.in

———

Let Your Soul Grow

Experience life-changing transformation—one video
at a time—with guidance from the world's leading experts.

www.healyourlifeplus.com